Up Sell Your Home

In Any Market!

James A. Harner

7/21/2012

It is so important to protect yourself if you are fed up with the traditional way of selling houses, or should I say the traditional way of **NOT** selling houses. Do you own due diligence – commit to reading this book and take it very seriously before choosing any type of professional representation in a real estate transaction.

It's time to take matters into your own hands.

It's *your* house, and it's *your* money.

Dedication

This book is dedicated to all those home sellers who are fed up with the traditional way of selling, or, I should say, the traditional way of ***not*** selling houses. Perhaps, like me, you contacted a big-name realtor, listed your home in the MLS for sale, and then waited. And waited. And waited. Then when it did not sell, it was somehow your fault and the only "solution" offered was to lower the price again, and again, and again.

If this sounds familiar, then this book is for you. It's time to take matters into your own hands. It's your house and it's your money. This book will show you how to do it.

Forward

I was skeptical when James first approached me about writing another "how to sell your home" book. I've consulted for top real estate brokerages like Prudential, Coldwell Banker, RE/MAX; developed internet marketing systems for top independent local brokerages; and educated thousands of real estate agents on marketing.

The PROBLEM - 95% of agents and brokers do NOT tell the truth to home sellers - or buyers - about what really goes on in the bowels of their dying industry. They don't know or hide market statistics and mislead their clients constantly about the effectiveness of trendy tech tools. They'll sell their clients out at the drop of a hat to make a quick buck. The way many talk about their clients with disrespect if not outright contempt is shameful. For all of the above - they blame you.

James book tells the truth. He cuts through the clutter in a personal way that reveals unique insights that you won't find anywhere else - insights that will help your home sell faster for more money and with less stress. James cares deeply about other people and tells the truth. You now have the information you need. What you do with it is up to you.

Samuel Ingersoll-Weng
Founder, Real Estate Consumer Education Foundation

Contents

Introduction

Don't do it! If you're like me (and lots of other people), you skip the introduction. Nothing important is ever in the introduction, right? Wrong! This time, I promise you will be in awe. You need to read it to understand how to benefit from this book. I'll keep it short and to the point, and I'll make it worth your time.

My name is James Harner, and I am Batman (more about that in a minute). I am the leader of a marketing revolution in real estate. I live by the "No Fear" principle in my life. I am the man, who other real estate agents, brokers, pretend experts and marketing gurus will knock as unfairly competing, yet will rip off and blatantly steal my original ideas and concepts, then repurpose them to appear as original ideas. I am 100% self-made and largely successful due to my own self-determination. I am a seeker of the truth and I am willing to share it in print.

I have long battled the Joker and the Riddler, enemies of the people using my superpowers of observation and action. I am also ..... no one special. I am a flawed human just like the rest, with just as many mistakes to my credit as successes. I have sacrificed a great deal to write this book. This book is intended to pull back the curtain and reveal the truth behind the lies of many real estate agents and brokers in residential real estate, aka the "Wizards of Oz", who dispense advice to homeowners causing continued failure and frustration to homeowners. Those agents and brokers advice is, at best, ineffective, at worst, criminally misleading and destructive. Yes, I am Batman.

I gather you're already forming an opinion about me. Maybe you hate me. Maybe you are starting to like me already. Maybe you are sufficiently interested to see where this book is going to lead you. What I can promise you is – by the end of this book – you'll either passionately agree with me and want to continue your relationship with me. Or, you'll passionately hate me. Either way I am fine with your decision. I have the skin of an Alligator and bluntly, I am not here to impress you. I'm here to tell you the unabashed TRUTH about real estate. I am not so disillusioned to think for one minute, the truth I present, will be respected by all. In fact there is probably a real estate broker somewhere sipping an overpriced latte, "hating" on me and thinking of rousing a lynch mob of brokers to silence the arrogant a-hole who has written this book.

So what's the truth? If you're reading this book, you are probably considering selling your house. You bought the book because you're doing research prior to selling or a friend was a real estate agent gave it to you to help you during was often the most stressful part of an already stressful time: packing up your life into a truck and moving.

I'll be honest. What you're about to read was not originally intended for you. It was intended for professional real estate agents. What I found out is that most professional agents, for the most part, don't get it! What amazes me is that consumers-people actually selling their homes-did get it! And why don't agents get it? Because it flies in the face of all the training they've received since they became agents. That's right, the public understands it, but the professional folks do not! Makes you wonder....

As someone who has bought and sold many homes personally and helped hundreds of customers sell their homes, I'm willing to bet you have only two primary objectives in your upcoming sale.

1. To make the most money you can.

2. Sell your house in the least amount of time.

Right? I thought so. The selling approach I'm about to share with you will accomplish both of your objectives.

It has a proven track record of selling houses in roughly half the time (57%) and netting (after all closing costs and expenses). The sellers who have used my up sell program gain an additional 3.9% more money than those sellers who don't. That **NET** profit to you!

Today there are over 2 million real estate agents in America, so I guess you could say that there are 2 million ways to sell your home. But the truth is that there is really only one way that is taught by the masses to the masses: selling your home by the price method.

There is an alternative…..

I am about to teach you how to Up sell Your Home by using the *"Active Marketing Method."* Every other sales method is a subsidiary of either one of these two methods. In this book we'll explore the two different methods at length and discuss how they differ and how one of them will yield far better results and make you more money. So get out a pencil or pen and make some notes. I believe that after you understand this strategy in detail, you'll agree that this is the best way to guarantee top dollar for your home, and at the same time, less stress and time waiting for your house to sell.

Ironically, I first discovered this method of selling houses as a seller and not as a real estate professional. I had a house to sell and I wasn't having any luck. The house was in excellent condition and priced competitively, at least that's what my real estate agent told me. It was in good condition, had a nice kitchen and bathrooms. Three nice sized bedrooms, hardwood floors, deck, a Florida room, and it was only a block from the ocean. The house was vacant, since I had relocated back to the Philadelphia area which made it easier to show. The real estate market was hot. Interest rates were good. My agent was one of the top agents in town with a reputable company with many years of experience in fact, they were recommended to me by an attorney friend of mine in town. And finally, I was in the process of purchasing another home, so I was motivated. I had a house with a mortgage payment and I wanted to buy another house that was a great deal and I needed to sell fast.

No problem, right? Wrong!

The house went on the market and sat. A month went by without a single showing. Then another, and another. I was calling my agent regularly to vent my frustration. Each time, her solution was to lower my price. After lowering the price well below the appraised value of the house with no success, I just finally decided to take matters into my own hands. We raised the price-a lot. Guess what happened? It sold within a week at full price, much to my realtor surprise. How did I do it? That's what this book is all about.

I urge you to pay very close attention as you read this short book. Not only will it make your home sale thousands of dollars more profit, but it will cut your selling time in have. You'll notice that I've broken the entire approach into thirteen sections. It is very important you understand each one. Understanding them will put money into your pocket and will sell your more quickly than you ever thought possible. Not understanding them could actually cause you to increase the time your home is on the market and drastically affect the amount of money you walk away with, cause you months of stress and possible problems at home as you wait for a potential buyer.

Yes, I do believe I am Batman. But I believe that you are too. I don't believe this because I have an extraordinary opinion of myself, I believe it, because adopting the role of Batman in my business, and utilizing Batman's mission as my own; protecting the citizens of Gotham City, has made me hundreds of thousands of dollars, and one of the top real estate agents in the country. In less than five years it helped me grow from being a single agent to being the leader of one of the largest real estate teams with Prudential Fox and Roach Realtors. I believe I am Batman because I understand who the real Batman character is; and how the role of Batman protecting Gotham City – is my personal crusade and business plan. Batman's cosmic role, above all else is an advocate for the little guy. This is why I have written this book. In a strange way, I’ve felt compelled to. This information exists nowhere else. No one else is talking about it. And before you jump to any foolish conclusions: Read this book. Get to know me. I am transparent. I am 100% authentic. I have no hidden agenda. You may end up hating me. You may also end up liking me. But make an informed decision, not one of impulse.

Never forget this, you're probably about to make some of the most important financial decisions of your life, so it's critical that you are well prepared. To that end, I offer you this approach - my approach - which is a proven and repeatable system, backed by market research –a revolutionary concept to selling homes 43% faster and for up to 18% more money in any real estate market, whether a buyer or seller market. You are welcome to use it to sell your home quickly and maximize your profits on the sale.

Thank you for reading, we welcome your feedback. Please, please, puh-leese! Feel free to contact me directly with your questions at this email: james@jamesharnergroup.com

Sincerely,

James Harner

Chapter 1:

A Brand New Approach to Home Selling

Desperation is the Mother of Invention

Back in the late 1990s, before I went into real estate, I lived in an incredible home a block from the beach in a quiet residential beach community. It was my "dream home," and I literally fell into the opportunity to own it by luck and timing. I could look out the back windows and see wildlife in the Seashore State park nature reserve just behind us. I could look out the front window and see the sun rising over the Atlantic Ocean and waves crashing on the beach. It was a typical beach home, built in the late '60s: single floor living. It was surrounded with homes on similar lots, of similar size, and some new luxury homes had been recently built in the last few years, which was a sign of things to come for this quiet residential beach community. Unfortunately for me, I owned it with my business partner. We were in the process of negotiating a sale of the company and we had to turn the property to a liquid asset . . . CASH! I called my corporate attorney for a real estate broker referral. Now if you have ever lived in the good ol' south, you would know that a lot of business is done through this type of professional "good old fashioned" network. The real estate agent, who was a she, came with an excellent track record, had many plaques and awards attesting to her sales performance, and was with a long standing brokerage in the area, known for listing beach homes. It seemed like a perfect fit.

We met at the house to discuss how best to sell it. It was clear she'd done her homework, and she brought sales data from several other homes that had recently sold in the area, as well as information about herself and her company. She'd prepared a comparable market analysis. *(Note: In real estate "speak," this is called a "CMA" and is a report that uses other similar sold properties to determine market value for the house in question. It is typically prepared by a real estate agent to advise a seller on how to price a home.)* The CMA suggested our house should be listed (more jargon, meaning "put up for sale") at $595,000. She loved the house, location, amenities, and the off street parking which is a big deal at the beach.

At this point you should understand that we'd recently had a professional appraisal done, for company purposes, which came in at 625,000. So needless to say I was surprised at her suggestion of a price so much lower than the appraisal. Nevertheless, since she was the "expert" and came highly recommended by my attorney, I went with her recommendation.

In addition I had a family member who was a real estate broker in the Philadelphia area. I asked him for his advice on what to do, since her CMA was 30,000 less than our bank appraisal. His advice was to find a good agent and price it accordingly and that sometimes bank appraisals were also incorrect. He said that appraisals were yet another's qualified professional opinion on value, but a buyer has the final say when it comes to "real value" in the market. I met the advice of the listing agent part of the way, and we agreed to list the home for 605,000. She assured us that even though, we felt that we were taking a 25,000 loss right off the bat, that this was a market price she could confidently sell the home at, without much negotiation.

In hindsight, this was the beginning of the best seller's market ever.

Well after a month and not a single showing, I called her and asked what was wrong. She suggested lowering the price to 595,000 since the market "had spoken." "Do you want to know what the market said?" she asked. I sure did! She told me it had said that we were "over-priced." Wow! Here we were in what was the beginning of the best seller's market that this area had ever experienced, with a home priced $30,000 below the appraised value, and we couldn't even get anyone to schedule a showing. She next suggested "staging the home," since we had moved out most of our furniture and personal belongings. I asked how much is that going to cost? She deferred and said, "I have an associate of mine who is a professional stager and has a natural gift for this kind of thing. I'll have her give you a call to discuss her process and fee structure." I thought to myself, "That sounds expensive!"

I was beginning to get frustrated. I needed to sell this home to be able to sell the company to my operating partner and her silent partner, but not being a real estate expert, I had to rely on the advice of a professional. I reluctantly lowered the price to $595,000, as she had suggested, and yet another month passed, again without a single showing. Why couldn't we get anyone to at least look at our home? Was this house a "dog?" HELL NO! It was picture perfect. It was in a prime beach location, in a quiet residential neighborhood, where everyone knows everyone. It was a corner lot, close to the state park and the beach. It had a two car garage, 3 nice sized bedrooms and central air. It has polished oak hardwood floors and a Florida room, deck and hot tub. The floor plan was open and very livable. The updated kitchen was large and spacious with lots of cabinets and Corian countertops. The house was beautiful by anyone's standards; it was vacant, making it easy to show. But, for some reason, it just wasn't selling, and I was getting more frustrated by the day.

After a third month with still no strong buyer interest, I asked my agent what she thought we should do. It came as no surprise that she suggested we have the home professionally staged and lower the price again to 575,000, to attract a fresh crop of buyers (remember that it had been appraised 4 months ago at $625,000). This time however, I balked. I was frustrated. How could she say that we had a price problem when we had only 1 showing of the home? I told her we didn't have a price problem, we had a *traffic* problem.

Because, I am a "tell it like it is" kind of guy, she was a bit taken back. Her next comment was, "Well if you have any great ideas, beyond what I've suggested, I'm all ears." I was on the spot. I felt that the current approach was simply not working and that something had to be done. My mind raced. I knew if buyers could just see the house, we would sell it.

Eureka I've Struck Gold

And then it hit me . . . how were buyers ever going to see my house? At this point the internet and online MLS was in its' infancy. Every buyer all had real estate agents, mostly from the same "old fashioned network," and their agents were helping them pick which homes to see. I realized that I was advertising to the wrong people. I needed to motivate the agents, not the buyers. I asked my agent what the buyer agent commission was. She said that we were offering a 2.5% commission to the agent who brought in a buyer. That is when I had what I refer to as an "AH-HAAA!" moment! I realized that we, meaning ME, were paying a total commission of 6%, with my agent receiving the big chunk of that commission! This was the reason no one was showing my home! After a little research I found out that most every home for sale offered at least a 3% commission to the agent who brought in the buyer, and ours was only 2.5%!

When I questioned her about this seemingly unfair split, she stated it was company policy to offer 2.5% on all listing contracts, with .5% going towards marketing cost (which meant to her) and the remaining 3% also going to her. I thought, "That isn't very fair to a buyer's agent. Why on earth would a buyer's agent want to show my house when all my competition was offering a higher commission?" I told her this buyer's agent commission was unacceptable and I wanted to try bribery, yes, bribery!

What a great idea! A big smile came across my face. I told my agent I wanted to raise the price to 625,000 (where it had professionally appraised earlier) and leave a copy of the bank appraisal out on the kitchen table. Then I wanted to raise the buyer's agent commission so we would effectively bribe agents to show the home. She hated the idea, thought it was unethical and would never work. I also said I would pay for the staging from her friend to the tune of $2,500, if she would hire a professional photographer to retake the pictures once the home staging was completed, at her expense, and produce a professional full color home pamphlet.

It was plainly evident that her strategy was clearly not working. I was the one making the mortgage payments on a vacant home. She reluctantly agreed to honor my requests.

And guess what happened? People miraculously started looking at the house the very same day the commission was changed. Once the staging was done and the new photos were updated on the local MLS listing service, we got a wave of showings, one right after the other. As I predicted, we sold the home in less than 2 weeks from there. Guess how much? You guessed it! For the full $625,000! We were ecstatic! And I was relieved. Did I have a price problem? NO! I had a traffic problem. And we were trying to fix a traffic problem with a price solution.

Lessons learned:

- Price alone does not sell houses.
- Agents also sell houses.
- If I wanted to attract buyers in droves, I had to attract agents too. It was really simple.

Was it a carefully devised marketing strategy? No. It was a knee jerk reaction to the utter frustration of having the perfect home and no buyers. Like the analogy that if a tree falls in the forest, and there is no one there to hear it, does it make a sound? Honestly, it worked then, and it's worked hundreds of times since then. It's as simple as supply and demand.

More Demand + a Fixed Supply = a higher price

Did I get lucky? HELL NO! It wasn't luck at all. It wasn't a fluke either. It was a basic premise of Economics 101 at work in my beachfront neighborhood. And it works in your neighborhood too. After that experience, I knew I had a secret weapon whenever I had a house to sell again. As it turns out, my family has a real estate brokerage in the Philadelphia area and I decided to give real estate sales a try after selling my interest in my former import and export company. I pulled out my secret weapon to sell my clients homes. The more I used it, the more I learned about how to maximize the results from it. In the years since, I have tweaked and refined the strategy until it is nearly perfect. And this very strategy – just as it's presented here – made me one of the top 1% of real estate agents in the country in a few years. My clients sold their homes in about half the time, well actually 57% of the time, of the local market average, and after paying all costs (including the increased commission/ethical bribe) averaged nearly 3.7% more money, NET! WOW! Half the time while netting 3.7% more money! That's the kind of result you should expect! Often much more using my advanced techniques, we'll discuss later.

So as we get into my home selling strategy, I want you to resist the temptation to dismiss this approach as being market specific. It's not. Now that I have shared this approach with over 9,000 agents around the world, I have sellers actually using it across the country in all kinds of markets to get the most money in the least time. And as long as there are buyers and sellers, it works. It works in buyer's markets, and it works in seller's markets. It works in low priced markets, and it works in high priced markets. It works because the law of survival of the fittest works the same everywhere – just like the law of gravity.

Chapter 2:

Real Estate Truth and Lies

The Dirty Laundry

Please listen closely. Here's what you must understand because knowing this and never forgetting this will save (make) you a lot of money and eliminate mountains of frustration in your next real estate transaction:

"Real estate agents are
100% commission based salespeople."

This means that if they don't close deals, they don't get paid. Zero, zippo, nada, income. I'm no anthropologist, hell, I've only ever been a salesman myself, but the only thing I can think of why this happens is – maybe it's got to be some kind of hardwired "Survival Mechanism." Regardless though, of why it happens, just know it happens – and you have a serious need to protect yourself. So before you go down to the local discount "real estate agent in a box" superstore and select your agent off the discount shelf, let's actually dive into some of the things you need to be aware of in today's changing times.

The real estate industry is changing drastically, and all the old rules are changing with it. What used to work is simply not working any more. You've heard the sayings "Dog eat Dog" and "Look out for #1"... I encourage you, in your real estate transactions, to do the same. In my opinion, greed really only amplifies the unethical characteristics of already shady and immoral people. But desperation, which is pandemic right now among agents, sadly, is a different beast. As I've witnessed lately, has the power to motivate even the MOST *ethical* people (agents) into doing, seemingly totally out of character, unethical, immoral, and disgusting things – things they'd never *normally* do.

Against popular belief, maximizing your profit IS NOT only about selling your home for more money. It IS minimizing the "loss" of falling victim to unethical, ill-qualified, and incompetent agents doing their best to "steal" your home sale. By utilizing the competitive art of power negotiating with every available technique and device against the buyer and buyer agent you can ensure to maximize your profits on your home investment.

And of course, because every transaction has two agents you must know how to protect yourself from both sides, knowing the "scams" they pull. I know this book, like Richie Roberts keeping the $1 Million in unmarked bills, has made me public enemy #1 to the real estate community *"...for airing their dirty laundry"* – but hey, this why our clients trust us so much, why we have been able to get such amazing results! And why they happily refer their friends to our proven Up Sell Your Home Program. So, if stepping on a few "political toes" upsets some folks, earns me "hate mail" from the crooks I expose – *Oh well!*

Whether you realize it or not, the biggest threat to your real estate sanity isn't the market – it's the 'moral compass of your agent!" It's no secret that real estate agents have an unshakeable reputation for shady deals, dishonest stunts, dirty tricks and monetary shenanigans.

George Orwell once said, "In a time of deceit, telling the truth is a revolutionary act." Consider this chapter my revolutionary act.

Here's why . . .

Maybe you've heard the story of Frank Lucas, maybe not. Chances are you know who Denzel Washington is. He played Frank Lucas in a Movie a called "American Gangster," does that ring any bells??? In the early 1970's Frank Lucas was a kingpin in the Harlem drug scene. He controlled the market with a product he called "Blue Magic" where he imported pure heroin from Vietnam in Military cargo planes carrying the deceased bodies of American servicemen and women. He cornered the market in the U.S. He retailed and wholesaled and "chopped it down" only slightly before selling it on the streets. Having no transportation costs at all, thus affording him the ability to sell heroin that was twice as pure for half the cost, thus eliminating the competition from the marketplace. He began selling it to organized crime nationwide; he became the first kingpin of the drug trade.

Now there's more to this story . . .

Russell Crowe was also in "American Gangster," playing detective Richie Roberts, one of the few honest cops NOT "on the payroll" of any of Harlem's drug lords, or even Frank Lucas. While other cops were "shaking down" drug dealers for cash, accepting bribes to turn a blind-eye, Richie's honesty, made him public enemy number one. Instead of keeping nearly $1 million of unmarked bills, he turned it in. Other cops saw him as a threat. He couldn't be trusted.

Richie could have cared less. He hated corrupt cops. He hated them more than the heroin dealers selling the "Blue Magic." And as Frank Lucas's empire grew, the more of these cockroaches appeared from the wood work, looking to cash in. Lucas hated this, hated them. In fact, when Richie finally brought down Lucas, the two, obviously on opposite sides of the fence, cooperated to nail their common enemy: corrupt NYC detectives. In the end, and nobody would have expected it, three quarters of

NYC's Drug Enforcement Division was arrested and convicted.

***Unethical, immoral, cheats, liars…
nobody likes them.***

And while that same sentiment is true in real estate, concerning unethical agents, I'd appreciate discretion. This book, like Richie turning the nearly $1 million of unmarked bills, puts me the line of fire. Personally I could care less. I have heard ethics violation cases and rule on the unethical acts of agents all the time. I am painfully aware of what type of egregious and nefarious activities my less than ethical fellow real estate agents participate in. But if enough of these unethical agents complain to the Real Estate Commission or the National Board of Realtors – **NO MATTER HOW TRUE ALL THIS IS** – they may attempt to force me to stop publishing this book, even though it is protected under the First Amendment of the Constitution. They may threaten to take my license, or in other ways, try to silence me from speaking out on these acts.

And that would be a shame.

But it won't stop me.

You see, nobody likes to admit corruption in their own "precinct." Do you think the NYC Drug Enforcement Agency ever commissioned their own internal investigation to crack down on their unethical detectives? No! Of course not. Why? Because it would look bad.

If not for Richie Roberts, catching Frank Lucas, and Lucas's equal and general hate for these detectives, who knows how it would have continued?!?!? Because there are a few bad apples out there, my personal advice is to arm yourself with as much information as possible about the dirty tricks and scams these dishonest agents try to pull so you can spot them a mile away. The problem is in knowing how to spot the scammers and what are the scams they try to pull.

That is why I've written this book - to give a tell-all account of the most common scams the bad apples like to pull so you can be on the lookout. You'll be the envy of your friends and family when they find out that you have the insider's secrets of the real estate business.

The Cold and Hard Truth:

Whether you're a buyer or seller, you better know what you are doing and how to "play the game" because if you get screwed, well, that's your own fault. How can this be? Real simple. Because the National Association of Realtors (NAR) is one of the largest special interest groups in the nation, with almost a million members each paying $300 dollars in dues a year. They have squeezed congress to write real estate laws in their favor. They also have a set of by laws that prohibit any "Realtor" from speaking badly about another "Realtor." What this means is that if you make a bad decision in a real estate deal, shame on you, that's your bad, not the other agents, and to make matters worse, you can't even speak badly about their business ethics. It's like a cult, that you dare not speak ill of another member or else be threatened with losing your ability to practice your very profession. You should have known better, how to have played the game better.

I ask you, "Is that a fair and ethical way to do business?" No. But you're on your own… like it or not, accept it or not, acknowledge it or not, fair or not, that's the reality of how this game is really played.

It's wrong.

Take a Pro-Active Stance

But that's why it's so important to protect yourself if you are fed up with the traditional way of selling houses, or should I say the traditional way of NOT selling houses. Do you own due diligence – and take it very seriously before choosing any professional representation in a real estate transaction. It's time to take matters into your own hands.

It's your house, and it's your money.

Please do not get me wrong, I am not suggesting all real estate agents are bad people, unethical, or even guilty of one or more things in this report – but many are. I've witnessed it. And I suspect, like the three-quarters of the NYC detectives found guilty, it may be a higher percentage than you or I would ever think to guess.

Who knows? Maybe you've have your own horror story.

Maybe all this resonates a bit too close to home . . .

. . . cuts a bit too deep. I certainly know plenty of good families who have been negatively affected by an unscrupulous real estate agent. In fact, for this reason, is exactly why a good number of Philadelphia area homeowners found their way to my Up Sell Your Home Program™ in the first place – to escape the "rat race" and risk of being put through the ringer.

And now with the current economic climate in the toilet and the real estate market the way it is, from my own experience, and what I'm seeing on a daily basis, it is only gotten (and getting) worse.

Generally, speaking I do not believe, as people say, *"Money is the root of all evil."* I believe, in fact, money in the right hands can do much good. Look at Bill Gates. How many billions has he donated, how many people has he helped? How many schools has he funded to be built?

AIDS medications has he provided? Computers has he donated?

Of course, and to be fair, every cloud with a silver-lining has a dark-underbelly. For every humanitarian like Gates there is ruthless, life-sucking criminal like Bernie Madoff, driven by greed. Who prey on the good nature of people for their own greedy gain? So you must ask yourself, especially now, when the market has contracted, the number of homes sales has declined sharply, in desperate times like these, where some 250,000 real estate agents nationwide, have already turned in their license since they can't afford to continue practicing. They have been forced by personal financial pressures to leave real estate, and are now working at Wal-Mart and Target.

And if they don't want to be next Wal-Mart greeter, what would make a starving agent making $20K a year want to tell you about the "deal killing" tidbits revealed in this book? Do you really think, just because they "say" they have a fiduciary responsibility to you, as their client, that your best interests trump their own self-preservation interests? The old saying rings true about desperate times requiring desperate measures.

Understand that it only takes 60 hours of required coursework to take the most state and national real estate exams. The bar is set so pathetically low; you don't even need a high school diploma as a prerequisite to successfully become a real estate agent. In fact, the B.A. from the University of Washington in Marketing that I have earned didn't even count in any way towards my licensing requirements. You gotta love that a high school dropout is considered an equal to a matriculated PAC 12 grad with a BA in marketing in the eyes of the Real Estate Commission. Just pony up the licensing fee, take the 2 classes, pass the test with a 70% proficiency and that is it, welcome to the wild, wild world of real estate sales.

One word applies: PATHETIC!

Chapter 3:

Death of the Traditional Real Estate Salesman

Traditional Real Estate is a Dead Dinosaur

Sadly, the traditional practice of real estate listing is a dead dinosaur walking. No, the reason for the sameness is obvious: the internet has Wal-Mart-ized real estate agents, lessening the importance of the role of a truly professional real estate agent.

According to a recent Harris Poll which surveys, complies and ultimately ranks America's professions based on public opinion, firemen ranked #1, just ahead of scientists and doctors. Where do you think real estate agents ranked? Guess? Keep going? Further down? A little more, further….. exactly DEAD LAST. Just below the Bernie Madoff's and Johnny Cochran's (RIP) of the world, stockbrokers and attorneys. Right this day, there are good, honest agents with high integrity and skill approaching potential clients, who they know could be helped – getting shunned, ignored, treated as peasants, wondering sadly, "WHY?! What is wrong with these people, don't they trust me."

It really is no mystery at all, is it? Thanks to the "legend" of real estate agents, what's been told and re-told, and therefore accepted by society as the truth:

- horror stories
- amateurish behavior
- under-trained
- overpaid
- pushy
- bossy
- annoying
- brute force selling

The unethical cousin of the "used car salesman" has earned real estate agents the reputation, like pit bulls, of a few bad apples. Like it or not the real estate agent community has been pigeonholed into a negative reputation. The uncomfortable truth is that agents are hated by the general public before they ever get a chance to speak a word. It is only getting worse.

I give no grand illusions about radically revolutionizing the real estate sales profession. I do believe myself to be a Batman type character, championing the cause of the hardworking American homeowner. I am a businessman. I am very pragmatic and strategic in my business plan.

And I happen to believe the more part time agents left behind, the better.

In today's technology based society, prospective real estate buyers can find and view virtually any property on the market, instantly, without the help of any agent, see multiple photos, view virtual tours, see full videos of the property; without ever getting out of their pajamas. For the vast majority, buyer's agents are seen as little more than a "necessary chauffer."

The listing side has become no different; there is an equivalent story of commoditization. Where consumers feel agents have little value in the sales process and the advent of .com Help U Get-R Sold websites where homeowners can list their home themselves and potentially save thousands by not paying a commission.

It sounds easy. Mostly because agents fail to deliver real value to their home sellers. Many agents have got lazy and have not adapted to the new technology revolution that is currently on top of them. Few actually have any copyrighting, photographer, videographer or home staging experience, and since homes no longer fly off the shelves, there are thousands of examples of poorly marketed properties that never sell.

Virtually everything being taught to real estate agents in seminars and sold to them in marketing programs, preached to them by "sales gurus" and pretend experts is all liked to the traditional real estate business model. A new model is necessary, not just a "better marketing" or “new media” idea. Don't get me wrong, marketing is necessary, and the better the marketing the more consumers will flock to view your property. The traditional real estate sales model is fundamentally flawed and only guarantees frustration and disappointment.

Usta-be Syndrome

To be fair, I suppose I should touch on my qualifications to make such a bold statement about my chosen profession.

It was not my intent to become a real estate agent - to go to college, sacrifice my college experience, study Friday, Saturday nights, to graduate with near a perfect 4.0 GPA from the highly respected Michael G. Foster Business School at the University of Washington - to ultimately end up in the dungeon of the LOWEST RESPECTED* profession in America . . . Real Estate (*source Harris Poll).

Quite the opposite, I planned to be an Environmental Engineer and work in Renewable Energy technology. I only got into real estate, because, and for no other reason, like a whole bunch of others . . . I was not able to “cut the mustard” on all the engineering washout courses like Calculus and Organic Chemistry. I failed miserably at Drexel University's School of Engineering.

So by default, I chose a business major (like most other engineering washouts) and I ended up transferring to the University of Washington, in Seattle Washington, because I also thought I could be a rock star! At the time, Seattle was the up-and-coming place to play music and I thought, "What the heck . . . finish my business degree and play music at the same time, maybe I'd end up getting signed to a major label and I'd never have to work in the corporate world ever!"

Then . . . as the years passed after graduation. . . .

I got infected with what I call "Usta-be syndrome."

As in I "usta-be" a with a top concert productions marketing company (you'll know the name if I said it, instead of being a rock star I ended up managing them).

Then I "usta be" an importer-exporter and retailer of jewelry with retail and wholesale accounts worldwide. When I sold that company I got into real estate by default.

And that's how I got here. Not knowing what to do next, since my family had a real estate brokerage, I said, "What the hell! I sold my beach home for top dollar, the real estate market is heating up, why not do that over and over again for others?"

I asked my brother-in-law, a former top agent a now real estate broker, how to go about getting into real estate. He told me, and 2 months later, after taking 60 hours of required coursework for state licensing, I got my license and passed the state and national real estate exams. Presto, I'm a real estate agent. Then I took the required "Realtor" (a "Realtor" is a member of NAR) classes, paid the fee, agreed to abide by the "Realtor Code of Ethics" and I got the "Realtor" designation and access to the MLS.

Chapter 4:

Only Two Approaches to Selling Homes

The Price Approach

I've read hundreds of books on the subject of selling real estate. Most of them stress how important it is for a professional real estate agent to try to build the listing side of the business in order to achieve success. For those of you unaware, "listing" is a real estate term used to describe seller representation in the sale of their house. The term dates back to the days when real estate peddlers would stand on the corner with their "list" of properties they had for sale.

Ironically, nearly all of the books describe a carbon copy approach, with only slight variations. Now the reason for this sameness is obvious: it's the way listings have been done since the very beginning of the real estate business. Sure, it's having less success than it once did, but real estate suffers from a lack of creativity and no one wants to abandon this age old approach and try something innovative that might not work. That is the fundamental difference between a commission based salesman and an entrepreneur. We've all heard the saying, "if it's not broke, don't fix it." Well I am here to say; it is broken, and I have to fix it to make a future for my family.

Necessity is the mother of invention! I am about to show you a better way! I'm not talking about a theory but a real honest to goodness alternative to the traditional approach. It works wherever it is tried, no matter what. There is actually a better way.

Let's first explore the age old "Price Approach" to selling homes so that you understand it completely and why it is a walking dinosaur.

The Price Approach

The price approach is the way 99.9% of real estate agents are taught to market homes for their clients. Maybe you've experienced it. If you've even sold a home and used a real estate agent, chances are you've met the dinosaur . . . we'll see if this doesn't sound familiar.

First, the dinosaur (aka, traditional real estate agent) is instructed to find the "reasonable range" of value of a property and then to urge their clients to price the property at the low end of the range. If the home doesn't sell within a month or so, the dinosaur is taught to ask their client for a price reduction. Then, if the property still doesn't sell, the dinosaur says to lower the price again, and again, and again, until eventually a buyer bites.

Think about it . . . the dinosaur is selling the house by *price* as the marketing tool. That's why the dinosaur continues to lower the price or wait for the market to appreciate to effectively meet the asking price.

Why This Approach is So Wrong

So what's wrong with the price approach? It's great for agents, since they place the entire burden of selling them home on the back of the seller (and in the seller's wallet). I'd say this is not so great a deal for the seller.

Another reason agents like using the traditional price approach is that they don't have to spend much money on marketing the house. They also don't have to spend a lot of time or effort devising a marketing plan or promoting the property because the price is doing the marketing and selling work for them.

There's no doubt this approach will work, of course . . . it's been working for decades with good and bad agents alike. However, there are a few serious drawbacks to the traditional price approach that are seldom mentioned to sellers.

Foremost is the agency issue. Agency is real estate terminology for: "who is the agent really representing or who the agent is working for." It's the job of the listing agent to represent the seller's interests, which include getting the absolute top dollar for the property. However, most agents don't get top dollar when they use this approach, and the reason is as simple as supply and demand. When there are fewer buyers interested in competing for a home, the sale price may need to be discounted substantially in order to attract sufficient interest.

In economics 101" with a bloated supply and a scare demand (i.e., fewer buyers), prices drop.

Another drawback to using this approach is the lack of speed: several months may need to pass before the price approach has time to take effect, simply due to the fact the agent is waiting for the seller to get frustrated enough to agree to reduce the price over, and over, and over again. In the process, the home usually gets stigmatized. After several price reductions, it's not even shown to potential buyers because it's been on the market too long and agents assume it has some potential flaw or defect that will make it unsellable. If the agent prices the home to high and reduces the price too slowly, the property becomes very difficult to sell at any price.

Many times the listing agents become de facto buyer's agents, actually representing the buyers' needs rather than their own seller's needs.

Playing both sides of the fence = Dual Agency

I'm honestly ashamed of the real estate industry and being associated with it, especially being that it condones such behavior – Dual Agency is perfectly legal in a Pennsylvania real estate transaction, and many other states as well. DUAL AGENCY is defined: "When the licensee works for BOTH the seller and the buyer. A dual agent may not take any action that is adverse or detrimental to either party."

Huh!? How the heck is that for an ethical dilemma?

Would the BAR Association ever allow attorneys to represent both parties in a legal action? HELL NO. Our Trial by Jury system would be the laughing stock of the free world.

If they did, don't you think your best strategies would be revealed and leave you with no "negotiating power" in the courtroom. You'd be powerless. Remember, loose lips sink ships and after all, agents are 100% commission based sales persons. So who do you think the real estate agent is looking out for if they are representing BOTH the buyer and the seller?

THEMSELVES, THAT'S WHO!!!!!! A Dual Agent will usually give away the farm to get both sides of the commission, or what is known in the biz as "playing both sides of the fence." It is entirely too easy with the traditional real estate listing approach to help the buyer rather than the seller. Counter to popular belief, this approach to selling homes is very common, if you'll honestly examine this method; you'll have to agree that, very often, it is not in the best interest of the seller.

Now, onto the alternative.

The Active Marketing Approach

To clearly understand the active marketing approach, we need to turn our attention to the term "reasonable range."

Valuing real estate is entirely different from valuing other common commodities. For instance, anybody can look up a share of stock and immediately see its current price. Or a gallon of milk - there is an established market price for milk that you get easily by looking at the supermarket. But because real estate values are subjective since there are many factors that determine price and there are no two houses that are identical, there tends to be about a 10% flexibility in the price range. Economists call this "price elasticity."

Consider a home that has a value at $100,000. It's not worth $100,000 exactly! It's really worth somewhere between $95,000 and $105,000. If the price drops below $95,000, nearly everyone will agree that the house is a good deal; and if the price goes above $105,000, nearly everyone will agree that the property is poorly priced, given the competing properties. However, within the "reasonable range," there is little price resistance.

Here's how the "active marketing" approach works:

Instead of listing the home at the low end of the range as we did using the price approach, we raise the asking price to the high end of the "reasonable range." Unfortunately this creates a problem. Now there's no compelling reason for any agent to show it. So, here is the solution to that problem: simply raise the commission.

Generally a small increase of only 2% is enough to make the difference. What you're effectively doing is bribing the buyer's agents to include your listing on their showing lists. I ask my seller clients to raise their commission from 6% to 8%, and then raise their price about 10% from the low end of the price range to the high end of the price range. The seller then nets about 8% more money before any negotiations and usually in about half the time that the price method would take.

Beautiful.

What about Appraisal Problems?

Sometimes, not often, the appraisal comes in short of the sale price, and the seller is faced with the decision: either reduce the price or lose the deal, assuming there is an appraisal contingency. When this happens, it's usually a minor adjustment. Similarly, the buyer also has the option of paying, out of pocket, the shortfall in the appraisal or canceling the deal if there's an appraisal contingency. In either case, when the house doesn't appraise for not just for sale price, seller is assured he got absolute top dollar for is home.

"But agents aren't supposed to let commission dictate what homes they show!" . . . yeah right!

Now, I know that most any agent will immediately say, "I never look at the commission when I'm working for a buyer," but I don't believe that noble sounding claim for one minute because statistics clearly indicate that is not true.

I don't know any agent who would willfully sell a client a home that wasn't right for him, but if there are 16 homes in the market that generally match the client criteria, and if 1 of those homes pay higher commissions than the rest, it's certainly not unethical to make sure that one with a higher commission is on every showing list. In addition, there's nothing wrong with an agent suggestively encouraging his client chooses to buy that one. If he doesn't, no big deal, but if he does at agent just got a big raise!

Why Not a Selling Bonus Instead?

One of the questions I'm often asked is why not just offer a bonus to the buyer's agents. Once again, the answer is simple: every buyer's agent knows that if he doesn't present a full offer, the first money to come off the table will be the bonus.

So the buyer's agent can find himself torn between getting the bonus and representing his client area if he advises his clients to offer less than the listing price, it goes without saying that his bonus is most likely out the window. On the other hand, if she encourages the buyer to pay the listing price, she's probably not representing the buyer's interests. For that reason, the selling bonus is often a guest incentive rather than a legitimate incentive to a buyer's agent.

Results speak for themselves.

While both approaches will sell your home, the fact is that the traffic approach will sell it quicker -historically, 43% quicker.

There is also another benefit: more money. After all expenses, including an additional 2% commission paid out to a buyer's agent, my sellers using the traffic approach have netted 3.9% more money.

How do I know? One statistic that we track is the "list to sale price ratio." This specific data tells us how much the typical seller ultimately discounts his home before it sells. Clients using this approach have had to discount their homes less . . . 5.7% less in fact. When you subtract the additional commission increase, you have a net benefit of 3.9%.

But what's really significant is that this decrease in price reduction is from a higher starting price (typically 10% higher). So while I can statistically prove a 3.9% net benefit, the fact is that in many cases, our clients net well over 8% more money after all expenses are paid. On a typical home that's over $30,000 more money – NET using the traffic approach.

An extra $30,000 in almost half the time?

Now isn't that a great reason to look closely at this active marketing approach?

Chapter 5:

Advertising Doesn't Sell Houses

Another Secret Exposed

Want to know another little secret? A secret your agent won't ever tell you?

Advertising doesn't sell houses!

You read it right . . . advertising does not sell houses. In fact less than 1/4 of 1% of all home buyers purchase a house they find in an advertisement. Less than a quarter percent advertising is simply not for selling house.

Okay, so why do we agents advertise then? Easy. Dinosaurs advertise to attract buyers. Let me explain . . .

In my market of regional Philadelphia, Pennsylvania, there are about 32,000 licensed realtors. The odds of any one of us selling our own listings is minor. While most agents would love to sell our own listings and earn both halves of the commission, with so many other agents looking for properties for their clients the chances of actually selling our clients homes are very small.

There are hundreds of other agents working with different buyers at the same time, and only one of them will ultimately find a buyer for our listing. But we still advertise our listing so that we can attract as many home buyers as possible. And will gladly sell those buyers any home - whether or not it is our listing.

Most agents have a simple philosophy: "focus on getting buyers, and the sellers listings will take care of themselves."

And that very attitude is largely responsible for the inability of most agents sell their clients homes, the fact is that nearly half the listings taken never go on to a successful sale. That means that half the sellers wind up not being able to sell their homes. In many cases the long wait exceeds the pain threshold of the sellers, so they decide not to move, or they're forced into making the home a rental property, or, even worse, they lose their home to foreclosure and permanently damage their credit in the process.

The reason that so few homes actually sell in a timely manner is that most agents simply don't have a marketing strategy or plan to implement of any sort. Their entire marketing efforts consist of simply:

- putting a sign in the front yard
- putting the home in the MLS (multiple listing service - the database of homes that real estate agents use)
- putting a lock box on the front door

- hoping the house sells.

Some will actually go as far as doing open houses and making flyers and hanging balloons. Then they proceed to find buyers and focus on selling homes while hoping someone buys their listings. Some eventually feel pressure from unsuccessful sellers and begin to advertise the listing - on average most realtors spend less than $350 to market a listing. Let's discuss some of those well-intentioned yet dumb ideas most agents allow themselves to be pushed into.

Real Estate For Dummies

What's amazing to me is, with all the supposedly "educated" Real estate agents in the USA, that these very same agents continue to purchase the next "shiny object", in hopes that they will attract a new crop of homeowners raising their hands to work with them. "For Dummies" book sales have exploded. I personally, would not be caught dead freely purchasing a book "for dummies". The majority of agents just *expect* buyers will see their ad in some real estate magazine and *want* to work with them, or visit their website and *want* to work with them. Such a "fairy tale" is not so. All agents suffer from "same marketing incest," and, lacking any knowledge of any real marketing strategies, they do what everyone else does.

If you need proof just open any copy of the real estate book you find. On every page you will see the same – all agents competing for the same fish, in the same pond, using the same bait. They see other successful agents doing this type of personal branding advertising, so they think that if they do the same thing they too will be successful.

WRONG! Brand advertising works for Coca-Cola, because they are a household name worldwide, with a product that is unique.

The Real Estate Book

A favorite place to advertise listings for sale is "The Real Estate book." These are generally publications that are distributed to the public for free, in rack locations at supermarkets, restaurants, and heavily trafficked areas like shopping centers. Home buyers pick them up as they walked by and, hopefully, are interested in the homes advertised inside.

There are 2 problems with encouraging your agent to use these magazines:

1. Readership of homes magazines has steadily declined over the past several years in favor of much more, complete and easier to search website listings. Because of that, the number of people

who call on anyone home has steadily dwindled to insignificance.

2. You need to keep your agent focused on selling your home, not running around showing homes to buyers and potentially trying to play dual agency on your property sale. Enncouraging your agent to advertise your home causes him to begin down the path of personal branding advertising to find buyers for his homes for sale.

Newsprint is Dead

Another favorite is the Sunday newspaper ads. Much like the Real Estate Book, these ads have become all but worthless as homebuyers have moved online to do their searching and shopping. Who even read newspapers anymore?

The real estate company I work under actually stopped printed newspaper advertising in 2012 completely due to its lack of return on the outlay of advertising dollars. Yes that's right . . . the 4th largest real estate company in the U.S. of A. stopped doing newspaper print ads!

You see there is the pesky little problem of time. The reality is that a single agent CANNOT give you their full attention if they are also running around with buyers to see homes and responding to buyer leads.

Open House Conundrum

This one has always been a puzzler to me. Not only does it almost never sell a client's home, but in this day of high crime it allows would-be thieves or assailants the opportunity to case potential victims. Not only is this a dumb marketing idea, but it is just plain dangerous. Every few months we hear about another seller who is either burglarized by a "potential buyer" while the home is on the market, or, even worse, is assaulted or even murdered by someone met at the open house. Please do not fall for this bad marketing idea.

Direct Mail Disaster

It doesn't get much dumber than this one. The problem is that with postage rates and printing costs as high as they are, and with most agents having a lack of understanding of who our target audiences really are; direct mail marketing pieces are read less and less since most agents have no idea how to write direct mail copy.

Direct mail has to be one of the biggest wasters of time and money for anyone besides the most savvy direct-mail marketers. Hand delivery is not much better when you factor in that time the agent stands doing it. This time would be much better invested to other agents. After all, it is the agents that sell houses, not advertising.

Another problem with this idea is that it focuses your agent on finding buyers, again taking their focus off of marketing your home properly.

Tell your agent that if they feel it necessary to send out flyers and postcards, send these to other agents please.

Selling Bonus Bait and Switch

This idea actually sounds very similar to the approach we discussed earlier but it's not the same the way it works is that the seller offers a bonus, for example, $2000, to the buyer's agent. The primary difference is that this strategy actually has very limited results, and here's why.

Agents all know that most selling bonuses never actually materialize. The reason is simple - very few homes are bought for a full price offer. And when negotiations began and the sale price is reduced, the first money to come off of the negotiation table is the selling bonus. The reason the selling bonus doesn't work while the increased commission strategy does; is that with the increased commission, that agent knows that if there is an accepted contract - at any price - you'll actually get paid the increased commission amount as opposed to having it disappear as soon as negotiations begin.

The fact is that nationwide over half the homes placed on the market never sell. The problem is not the homes. I can tell you from experience that I've sold some of the most unattractive homes using this simple approach, while I watched as many of my colleagues had very nice listings sit on the market for months without so much as a solid lead. I watched as they focus their efforts on advertising and attracting buyers and ultimately don't get the top job done for their selling clients.

Why? Because advertising doesn't sell houses, agents sell houses. But maybe you don't even need an agent at all. In the next section will discuss whether or not hiring an agent is the best plan for selling your home.

Chapter 6:

Use and Agent or Go FSBO?

Can You Wear the Shoes?

Okay, we've talked about what not to do in the way of advertising, and we also talked about a method that will sell your home in half the time while netting you as much as 10% more money in the process. Now let's talk about the whole subject of whether or not to hire an agent.

I've already told you that I am a licensed real estate agent, so you would expect what I have to say to be somewhat biased. Maybe it is. But let me start by making a very bold statement:

I don't think every seller
needs an agent to sell a home!

Let me make another seriously bold statement while I'm at it:

I wouldn't list my home with
90% of agents that I've met!

I have a very simple philosophy when hiring agents to work on my team (or when hiring any assistant for that matter): if the agent can't add more value to the transaction than what I pay him, they are a bad investment.

Nothing personal, it's just business to me. If the agent were an employee, I would want him to add more value to the company than what I pay him a salary. A real estate transaction is the same. There simply hiring someone to represent you in selling a large asset - often the most valuable asset you will ever own.

So should you hire an agent or sell your home yourself? That shouldn't be a difficult decision. It should be very easy. And the decision should be made on the basis of whether or not an agent will make you more money than you pay him. I can say that national statistics actually show that using an agent to sell your home will yield 3 to 11% more money on average. But how can you know for sure if you need an agent? And if you do, in fact how can you best determine which agent to higher in the virtual sea of agent mediocrity. After all, the majority of agents in the marketplace aren't even looking out for their seller, they are looking out for themselves and attracting more buyers. However, selling yourself can be a hair-raising experience with shady offers from seasoned investors and con artists, inaccurate title reports and conveyance nightmares(the term to describe the accurate accounting of leinable utilities and mortgage payoffs).

There is a serious learning curve that doing for the first time there are bound to be mistakes made. Any seasoned agent will more than earn his or her commission while keeping your life relatively stress free by managing all the details for a successful closing. Think of a really good agent as an air traffic controller, who manages all the incoming traffic and sees that your plane lands safely at the settlement table.

The Correct Mindset

First, let's get our mindset adjusted correctly. The goal here is a very simple one: it's a matter of finding one single buyer unit . . . a single person, a couple, or a family. We need just one, but the aim is to get the one that is the best, that is the one who can give you the highest price and the best terms, to close within your timeframe.

Well, I have good news!

There is really only one criteria that must be used in making a decision: "What is the average days on market (DOM in real estate terminology) for homes in my community?" To make an educated decision about selling your home by yourself, you must know the answer to that simple question.

The Key to Success

If DOM is below 60, the economic climate probably exists successfully sell your home for top dollar on your own.

It is as simple as that. If DOM is over 60, you will likely be among the 91% of for sale by owners who never successfully sell their home. If the economic conditions are not right, the FSBO seller is simply at too great a disadvantage to compete in a buyer's market when the buyers are looking to save the same commission that the seller is attempting to save by selling it alone.

There's a problem with finding accurate DOM statistics, however. Where can you get access to that information? The best place to get that information is from an agent. He should be able to log onto his local MLS database and get it for you. But here's the real underlying problem: normally, the number given to you will be an inaccurate DOM number that has been invariably skewed lower than what the real number is.

Don't misunderstand me? Say you are given by the agent the DOM number that is reported in the local MLS, but that number is not the correct number because it is only the average days on market for houses that actually sold. It does not take into account those homes that did not sell or those that were listed several times before they ever sold, or the listings withdrawn from the market, or the builders models that were never listed until a contract was written.

Whew!

So how can you know what the real DOM number is? Is it possible to determine the actual DOM for your market even if you're not a rocket scientist? Absolutely! Just use the absorption rate to calculate the true DOM for your area.

Let me show you how to do it here's how you go about finding the current DOM. You need two pieces of information:

1. You need to find out how many homes sold in your local market last year.
2. You need to know how many homes are currently available on the market as active listings.

Any agent should be able to get these numbers for you.

For example if 12,000 homes sold last year, and there are currently 1000 homes on the market, what those numbers indicate is that the current inventory level turned over 12 times last year (12,000 divided by 1000 equals 12.0).

Now, 12 (the number of months in a calendar year) divided by times turned equals the market absorption rate (given in months).

Here's the calculation:

12 divided by 12.0 equals 1.0 (the absorption rate)

This means that the average home was on the market for 1 month. So to convert the absorption rate to DOM you simply multiply absorption by 30(1.0 x 30 = 30).
By calculating DOM this way, you'll get an accurate DOM number, and eliminating any manipulation of the DOM by agents who relist stigmatize homes as well as inaccuracies caused by those listings that never sold and were withdrawn and relisted by a different agent. In the above example, the market condition is such that it is a seller's market, and it might make sense to try to go it alone.

This is exactly the kind of market that several of the hotter regions were experiencing right at the height of the housing bubble.

I remember having an agent friend tell me about his market, Seattle, in 2005. It was so hot that is seller could put a sign in his yard, run an ad in the local newspaper, and opened his home for viewing for only one day. Buyers (with and without agents) would all bid for the house at the same time, and many would write offers and submit them during a two-day opera window, many with escalation clauses. At the end of that time, the seller would select the best of the offers, many of which would be higher than his original asking price. The escalation clause would push up the sale price even higher in a bidding war to a maximum amount the buyer was willing to entertain in order to see they got this particular home.

In a market like that, you certainly don't need an agent to find a buyer; nevertheless, in many cases having an agent might still be wise simply because a good agent should be able to more than earned his feet by his ability to negotiate real estate transaction, his knowledge of creative deal making, and more importantly, his knowledge of the traps many sellers unwillingly fall into that ugly cost them tens of thousands of dollars.

Now let's look at another example.

Let's say 12,000 homes sold last year and there are currently 6000 homes on the market at the same time this year – this means that the inventory turned twice last year (12,000 divided by 6000 equals 2.0). Take it a step further . . . 12 (months) divided by 2.0 equals 6.0(the absorption rate), then the time the average home is on the market is now a full 6 months.

We convert the absorption rate to days on market by multiplying absorption by 30(6.0 x30 =180). In this case, it would be almost impossible for even the most talented and motivated seller to successfully sell his own home. The market climate just makes it too difficult to swim against. The market is no longer being controlled by sellers. In this scenario, only a foolish seller would even remotely consider FSBO.

Chapter 7:

Preparation is Key to Successful Selling

Viewing Your Property as a Product Launch

It is simple fact that when you have 2 products equal in price, function and quality, the better looking property will outsell the other 10 times over. Whether you're selling your principle residence for a fixer upper, you should have a sparkling clean property to sell before you put it on the market.

You must ensure that your property stands out from the other listings if you want to sell it quickly. It must make a strong, positive first impression. It is a fact of psychology that all humans remember visual impressions first and foremost, and then they react emotionally. Humans back up their first emotional impressions with rational thinking later on. The good news is you don't have to spend a fortune to get your home stand out from the crowd.

Property Preparation Can Help Speed Your Sale

Before putting your home on the market, you need to decide how much you're going to spend on time and labor to get it ready with market. Before doing so, you need to look at the other houses in your area and do some homework first.

If you plan on asking the same price as your competition; which offers a completely renovated kitchen and bathrooms, you had better make sure your kitchen and bathrooms are also updated. If you decide that renovating your kitchen is out of your budget, then you either have to price your house accordingly or have some other selling features that offset and justify the comparable sales price you're going to ask for your home.

Without getting into a discussion about full renovations and rehabs, let's just discuss the necessary items in order to present your home in its most favorable light.

- Cosmetic updates may be a good idea if you have pets or small children. Cosmetic updates are generally paint, carpet, and a few choice items that give it to appeal. Your budget will depend on the size of your house, but generally $3,000-$5000 should be enough. Reality TV shows on the HG TV channel such as Sell This House are good to watch for ideas. While the budget stated on the show are a bit unrealistic sintering what current labor costs are in the mid-Atlantic region, it does help you to focus on the most important aspects of creating the necessary appeal with the least amount of money.

- Paint and carpet go a long way toward sprucing up a dated home. Stick with colors that are warm, but neutral. Never use white or off-white as it is dull and boring. Soft tans, greens, and blues can be used with an offsetting off-white trim.

- If your doors are cheap, cracked or old and dark, consider updating with new six panel off-white doors with contemporary finished door hardware.

- Overspend on the small items that are not expensive in the entire scope of project. For example, if you only need 3 light fixtures in the house, consider spending $100 rather than $20 each. If you have two bathrooms, spending $100 per faucet will make a bigger impact than a $20 per faucet, but will only change your budget $160.

- Avoid overspending on items that don't produce appeal. While quality products will appeal to the logic of a buyer, it will not persuade him to buy as much as things that create emotional appeal. Expensive roofing, new furnaces, and hot water heaters don't make the house look any nicer. In fact, you should not replace any of these items unless they're "completely shot." If you replace the carpet, don't bother with expensive stain resistant products that cost extra since it is something that goes unnoticed to new buyers.

Professionally Staged Homes Net More Money

Staging your property is a necessary evil whether or not you update your property. It is a proven fact that staged homes sell for more money than us homes that are not staged.

If you're unfamiliar with the term staging, let me introduce you to this topic. In my opinion, this is going to be the single most important thing you can and will you get your home sold quickly or more money. Staging is basically showmanship. Staging is basically doing all the things that are necessary for making your house stand out from your competition. If properly staged, your house will stand out from the crowd, and people will pay more for it. If you do a great job of staging your home, you don't have to be a salesperson; you're a showman, and your house will sell itself.

You need to create some appeal to make your house stand out from the rest of the properties available for sale in your new. If you have ever considered new construction and have visited a builder's model home, you undoubtedly have seen staging at work. Since most people have very little imagination, a staged home helps people imagine what their things look like they go into the, even if their furnishings look completely different. Staging keeps the buyer saying, "YES!" and keeps all the "No's" out of the buyer's mind.

Staging always starts with curb appeal. Walk all the way around your property and make sure there are no visible trash cans, recycling bins, garden hoses or other eye sores. Don't ignore anything that takes away from your properties like new appearance. The outside appearance of your home is your calling card, think of it as a business card for your house. It is where all first impressions begin and end. Look for additional ways to create curb appeal:

- Add flowerpots, hanging flower baskets, or perhaps wreaths or pine boughs during the holiday months
- Make sure you pressure wash the exterior of your home and Windows.
- Replace any cracked or fogged windows. If you don't replace them, the property inspector will point them out and you'll end up crediting the buyer later on.
- Sweep the roof.

- Clean the gutters. While on the roof, look for torn shingles, were other things that need attention like a chimney.
- Water the lawn, remove any leaves, mow and edge your sidewalks.
- Remove dead flowers, fruit all shrubs and trees and be sure to add new colored mulch keeping a fresh appearance in the flower beds.
- Make sure the house is an inviting place to enter. The walkway to the front door should be well lit. If there is a dark or potentially unsafe approach to the front door, you should add the voltage lighting or solar lighting. It does not have to be elaborate or expensive. Just place 6 to 10 solar powered lights along the sidewalk, so visitors can see where they're going.
- Make sure the doorbell ringer is lighted and that it has a pleasant tone. Many buyers like to ring the doorbell before entering. Don't let them start their tour by finding a broken orbital.
- Check all the entry doors to see that they were properly. Buyers will not tolerate the doors with large gaps or difficult to use key holes, all of which are first impressions.

- Make sure there is a nice doormat placed at each entrance to welcome visitors – it will also help protect carpets in messy weather showings.

Now it's time to prepare the inside of your home.

Avoid the Seven Deadly Sins Home Preparation

Start by making sure everything is cleaned from top to bottom.

Failure to do so is deadly sin # 1!

- Wipe down all woodwork and cabinetry with Murphy's oil soap.
- Polish or wax hardwood floors.
- Remove all the dust from vents, ceiling fans, cabinets, and horizontal surfaces.
- If there are any spots or dullness or wear and tear, on the carpet, have them professionally cleaned.
- If there is a fireplace run the shop-vac and clean it thoroughly.
- If you haven't done so already, replace the old thermostat with basic programmable model.
- Walk through the house is quiet time and listen first week the floors or any other sound. Eliminate.

- Make sure every light bulb in the house is working.

Failure to de-clutter the house is deadly sin #2!

If you're still living in the home, start by de-cluttering the house of at least 1/3 of your personal furnishings at a minimum. You should plan on renting a pod storage unit and clear out a lot of the items your kitchen cabinets, closets, and garage and make it look more spacious. Remove any extra tables, sofas, chairs or personal collections.

Rearrange the furniture so that there is a nice flow between rooms, removing anything that awkwardly blocks your path freely flowing program through. Any loose electrical wires, computer cords, or other messy cables are a no-no. These should also be removed. Any paperwork, clothing, exercising equipment, toys, or other loose items should be moved into storage or out of sight.

You want to give the appearance that your house is spacious and free from clutter. A messy and cluttered house full of small items and disorganized papers is unattractive. You will effectively turn off most of your potential buyers. Remember, their current home is probably too small and cluttered they won't want to move into a similar environment!

Failure to remove personal items is deadly sin # 3!

Any home décor should remain relatively neutral, just so you have some color and texture when possible. Wall hangings, curtains, and artwork add personality to your own. Try to maintain a consistent decorating style that complements the architecture and engage him bosses, bold jewelry and candlesticks are just a few ideas items found in nature like dried flowers and pinecones, along with other items can be placed almost anywhere. All of these items can be moved from the home you are selling your next house you purchase.

Remember that first impression that is made when someone enters your home cannot be erased! If the floor is dull, add accent rugs and maybe a small table to change the focus. The table should contain a nice Plexiglas holder with information about the property and a place for real estate agents leave the business cards and maybe a candy dish.

In homes with floor coverings other than carpeting, you use throw rugs in all rooms. With beautiful hardwood floors, the rugs should be used as accents, while larger rug should hide unattractive floors.

If there are no overhead lights in the bedrooms or the living room, try adding a few floor standing lands. Keep the lights on at all times, and making clear that the house lights are to be left on after showing the home. In fact you can make a house a whole lot nicer simply by experimenting with different varieties of light bulbs in all the right places.

Out-dated wallpaper is deadly sin #4!

And definitely remove all wall paper! There are few buyers in today's market that like wallpaper. I suggest considering removal and repainting these rooms, lest you commit deadly sin number four.

A dirty kitchen commits deadly sin #5!

The kitchen is the heart of a home, all major discussions and decisions are made here. Make sure the stove oven and refrigerator are all completely clean or risk committing deadly sin number five. An unsightly fridge can really detract from the kitchen, so consider replacing the fridge if yours is an oldie. If your house is vacant, place some small decorative settings throughout the kitchen countertop, like a wine bottle and glasses and silverware and napkins, or a coffeemaker, just to give the suggestion of things and to provoke great memories the buyer's have stored in their heads.

Remember these settings will give a nice warm look to the home without having to go overboard decorating.

Nasty, dirty bathrooms! Yuck, and deadly sin #6!

Bathrooms should be spotless or risk losing a buyer.

- Always have matching towels and accents and a pleasant scent with candle plug-in air freshener.
- Buy an attractive shower curtain, for just a few dollars a colorful shower curtain can be had, and it looks great!
- Make sure there is no mold or mildew anywhere.
- If your bathroom is cluttered with personal care products, make sure you clear them out before showing the home. In a home is vacant, add a few items that look warm and inviting, such as candles in the master bath and a rubber ducky will add flair.
- A colorful throw rug on the floor of a like color will distract from any old style tiles that need replaced that are outside your budget.
- If you're going to invest the money in any bathroom, focus on the master bathroom first as this is the most important bathroom in the house when showing to prospective buyers.
- Add a few wall hangings, a few pictures, and a mirror or two in the bathroom as well as throughout the house, one item each bedroom

and at least two in the kitchen and family rooms. Don't use cheap looking artwork.

OooO that smell! Deadly sin #7!

Do not underestimate the power of smell or commit deadly sin number seven! It's essentially the lasting impression in everyone's mind. You want potential buyers to associate a pleasant fragrance with your property, even if that association is on a subconscious level.

Start by neutralizing any existing unpleasant or musty smells created by mildew, garbage, or pet odors.

If possible, open all windows during the final few days reparation, and he air moving throughout the house. Sprinkle a little baking soda throughout the house, leave it for several days, and then vacuum it up. Lastly, use natural air freshener such as fresh-cut flowers fresh pine quality potpourri. Plug-in air pressures also work well particularly in bathrooms.

Also, consider playing some soothing music in the house your showings deranged, soft jazz, classical music can create a different ambience. You can even have different music playing the parts of the home to stir up different feelings for the buyer.

Don't forget to inspect the basement, attic or other unfinished areas. Add lighting for these areas. Make sure they're completely clean. It is surprising how many listings have construction debris and other unsightly items lying around. It's fairly common to see what appears to be a well prepared listing, and then, upon visiting these unfinished areas, make unpleasant discoveries. A few examples include sewer line debris, mousetraps, dead animal remains, central air ducts, construction debris, cigarette butts, and drawers full of sawdust.

Your goal should be to show "up" every space in the best possible light. The only evidence of renovation should be well marked cans of paint, spare shingles, and similar items in an appropriate place.

Also worthwhile will be to have an area for display of product warranties, sprinkler systems, floor plans and even winterizing instructions. These items are typically on a table or counter along with other information regarding the property, loan options, homeowners' association information and other positive information about the neighborhood.

Make a Lasting First Impression

Keep in mind that people have been driving around your zip code and looking at anywhere from 2 to 20 homes, so you better make sure your home makes a great and lasting first impression. How is a couple who has been looking at 20 homes before finding yours going to remember yours instead of those other 20??? They all start to look alike after the first few showings, unless yours is a stand out.

Your home simply must stand out from the crowd, make it unforgettable. As you can see by the recommendations above, you don't necessarily have to spend a lot of money to make your house look like a model home. We call these emotional anchors; you are creating a memorable experience that reminds people of a happy time in their life, so buyers are more likely to remember your house. Emotional anchors are inexpensive, fun and creative, so use them as much as you can throughout your house.

Again, the idea is upgrade the appearance of the property, so don't use cheap looking items. You may feel qualified to make all decisions regarding your décor but it would be wise to get second opinions from interior decorators, or real estate experts. Visit model homes in new neighborhoods to gather ideas. You can even borrow a few items from your friends and relatives but nothing with too much sentimental attachment.

There are professional staging companies that will decorate the entire house, even bringing furniture with them. Depending on the size of the house and the price range, this may make sense. In addition virtual staging can also be accomplished or fraction of the cost of the physical staging. It will only appear attractive online, so it is not as valuable, but in an investment flip or relocation situation, it is much cheaper than furnishing the entire home and staging it. It is not uncommon for a full home staging to cost upwards of $10,000 for a million-dollar vacant home.

Keep it clean!

Lastly, remember that property showings require continued cleaning to maintain a presentable appearance. Properties that have been renovated will continue to show residual dust left standing on doors and drywall. Some listings have signs asking buyers to remove their shoes. While this practice in essence points out clean or new carpets, it doesn't invite potential buyers to make themselves at home. Builders showcasing immaculate homes don't ask such things and buyers, and it's not recommended by me in any way that you ask a potential buyer to remove their shoes. It simply, in America, is just not a cultural standard practice.

Again unless you are up to the task of staging your home yourself, you might consider hiring a staging professional there are various levels of staging, from all out furnishing the entire home top to bottom to small, decorative arrangements. You should interview several people to get a feel for how you can work with someone. Make sure that your staging professional has experience in selling homes that are similar in location, price range, and style to yours. Ask for references and a portfolio of pictures.

Chapter 8:

Researching the Competition

Do You Know Enough About the Market in Your Area?

Most sellers made a colossal mistake of not knowing the facts about their market before proceeding with selling their home. This is the primary reason why they fail miserably and end up with their home unsold.

One of the most important things you can do to get your house sold is to learn your market. This includes learning the current value of your property. Who is your competition and exactly what they are offering for sale in comparison to your home? Most sellers and real estate agents operate in the dark; simply offering the property for a certain price without regard to what other houses have sold or without regard to what other homes for sale are priced at.

The reality in today's marketplace is that consumers, aka, YOU, have access to just about every property for sale by numerous websites like Zillow, Trulia and Realtor.com. This allows consumers to window shop multiple photos and descriptions of every property in the price range. These sites may not provide an accurate opinion of value, however, it doesn't take a rocket scientist to figure out that when a property offers less amenities and upgrades than the competition and is priced the same, well, it is overpriced.

The primary danger of undervaluing or overpricing your home is that it can cost you tens of thousands of dollars, months of sleepless nights, arguments and utter frustration. If priced too low, people may think something is wrong with it, or even worse you'll let your hard earned money fly out the window to the first buyer savvy enough to recognize a good deal when he sees one. If priced too high, nobody will be interested enough to even make it past the online advertisements. They simply won't even make it to your front door.

The Macro View of the Market

Potential real estate sellers need to think about three specific areas in order to determine correct pricing:

1. The first dimension is the overview of the general market in your area.
2. The second is how your specific property stacks up against the competition in the market.
3. Third is the amount of time you have available to achieve the goal of selling your house.

For example, if your prevailing local market conditions are such that the number of sellers far outweigh the number of buyers and you have only a month to get your house sold, and obviously great efforts and aggressive pricing, along with avoiding mistakes, will be necessary to get to the closing table quickly. Furthermore if your property lacks uniqueness; then creativity and active marketing outside of the box, along with physical improvements to the property, will certainly be necessary.

Think Outside the Box

Let's just say for arguments sake that your local market is flooded with 4-bedroom homes competing with your 4 bedroom house. It may be worthwhile to convert a family room or second living room into another bedroom, assuming codes permit this. How many five-bedroom homes exist in your marketplace? This would be a good question you would like to know the answer for that may help finding a buyer who needs more than 4 bedrooms, where the marketplace offers none you would fill an immediate need.

Knowing the preferences of buyers in your marketplace is a critical key to success when planning your approach to marketing your home. It's not in any way about your likes, tastes and desires or preferences, but rather about what's hot and what is not.

Before we get into establishing the value of your particular property, it is important to take an overview of surrounding market conditions. Getting the macro view data is something that you can ask of a real estate agent or appraiser since they often use this information anyway. Market trend information can also be obtained through third-party resellers if you're choosing to sell your home yourself - Altos.com is such a source.

Days on Market Indicator (DOM)

The average days on market is critical for several reasons:

- it is important in setting realistic expectations about the time needed to sell a home;
- it will help you evaluate any operative command and make an educated decision about whether it's advisable to wait for another offer or to take what is being offered on the table; and,
- if you know the DOM for your market (or, better yet, for the specific neighborhood), you'll be able to make a better decision on pricing and negotiate accordingly.

There is a major problem with DOM statistics, however. Most MLS databases have a very inaccurate DOM number which is invariably skewed lower than the actual real world number. So how can you know what the real number is? Is it possible to determine? Absolutely! By using the absorption method to calculate the true DOM for your area, is how to arrive at the accurate number. Refer to pages 53 - 57 for a discussion on how to calculate the true days on market for your area.

Why the DOM Number in the MLS is a Lie

You may ask, why such a huge disparity in actual DOM number versus the reported number? Because the MLS calculates the average DOM as the average days on market for only the listings that *actually sold*. But as I stated previously, MLS completely leaves out of its calculation homes that are withdrawn, listings that expired, listings that were withdrawn and relisted (which restarts the clock, a typical real estate agent trick to make a home look like it just became available), or those that were never put in to the MLS until they sold (like new construction homes where they might list only one home in a subdivision, but actually have 400 for sale). All of these affect the real DOM number.

Absorption Rate- Extremely Valuable Information

The absorption rate is an extremely useful indicator of supply and demand for homes in your area. The absorption rate is simply a ratio of the number of homes for sale in your area divided by the number of closings in the last 30 days. By area, I typically define as a school district, since the school district determines how desirable a particular area ultimately is. It helps you estimate the number of months it would take to sell your home.

To figure out the absorption rate, we first need to decide on the boundaries of your local market, which again, I recommend the defined as a school district. A professional appraiser or top producing real estate agent rarely looks at houses outside a particular school district and so should you heed this same advice.

When you ask a real estate agent how long it will take to sell your home you need this critical data in order to accurately understand the market supply as it affects the number of homes buyers have to choose from. The number of houses currently for sale in your school district will be the numerator in your ratio. This is the supply figure. The denominator is the number of houses that sold in the last 30 days. "Sold" is defined as a closed transaction.

Once you divide the number of homes for sale by the number of sales in the last 30 days, you have the absorption rate, which is another way of saying the number of months that it will take to sell all the homes within your defined school district at the rate of homes are currently selling.

For example, if 60 houses are for sale and 10 have sold in the last month, then the absorption rate is six. Thus, if no other houses went on to the market, it would take 6 months to sell all the current inventory listed.

An absorption rate of 6 is a market in which sellers and buyers are balanced and equal force. Below that marker, the market is all the better for sellers, hence the term "sellers' market." The greater the absorption rate is above 6, the better the market is for buyers, which indicates a "buyers' market." Understanding the absorption rate and its trend over the last few months (whether trending up or down) can make sellers tens of thousands of dollars and a save great deal of time.

The absorption rate is to the seller is what GPS guided navigation is to a driver! It is hard to imagine navigating the housing market without this critical statistic.

Knowing your absorption rate conditions is the first step toward the right mindset when needing to get a home sold within a particular time period. I refer to the absorption rate as: a theoretical amount of time that it will take sell all the homes on the market at the current rate of closed transactions. In real estate, pricing the property with an eye on the supply quotient and a greater market forces is key to avoiding the unrecoverable mistake of mispricing a house when it first goes on the market.

Determine the Odds of Selling Your Home in Any Given Time

The next piece of market data I want you to learn is the "standard deviation of the average days on market." "What?!!" you say! I know what you're thinking, "Mr. Harner you have lost your mind! Standard Deviation?!"

Before you dismiss this concept (and me) as crazy, let me point out that it will be an easy statistic to calculate and a powerful advantage once you know the answer. What if you could actually know the odds of selling the home in 30 days, 60 days or 90 days? Wouldn't that make your life a lot less stressful? If I had a dollar for every client that asked me "How long do you think it will take to sell my house?" I'd be a very rich man.

There are 2 pieces of information needed to make this calculation:

1. First, you need the actual DOM for the area.
2. Then you need a standard deviation of that DOM.

I hear you . . . "The standard deviation of the DOM? How in the world can I calculate that?!" Trust me, it really isn't that hard to figure out . . .

Watch this:

An easy way to calculate the standard deviation of the DOM is by using a spreadsheet like Excel. Pull out all the closed residential properties that were your community in the last year from your MLS. Then copy and paste the data onto a spreadsheet. Then use the formula in Excel to compute the standard deviation with DOM column. If you're using Excel function will like this: =stdev(b1:b2000)

I'll give you an example. Let's assume the actual DOM is 240 (like right now in my market) in a matter of a few clicks here the odds of a home selling:

30 days- 10.1%

60 days-13.7%

90 days-18.3%

120 days-23.4%

150 days-29.3 %

180 days-35.8%

210 days-43.1%

240 days-50% (Remember, this is the average DOM)

270 days-56.9%

300 days-64.2%

330 days-70.7%

360 days-76.6%

390 days-81.7%

420 days-86.3%

450 days-89.9%

480 days-92.7%

Now let's say you invited a real estate agent into your home for a listing presentation and he tries to convince you that he can sell your home in a matter of days. *You tell them with complete certainty that the chances of selling your home in a few days are nil, and in reality you are mentally prepared for at least an 80% probability, using a traditional pricing approach.* That realtor will probably never bother you again, because you have produced facts that he doesn't even understand, nor was he ever trained to learn an advanced concept like this.

Average Markdown (Original List vs. Sale Price)

You need to be aware of the typical "discount" in your market. This is just like in car sales with the sticker price is not the price you walk out the door paying for the car. Let's see how this plays out in real estate . . .

Let's assume an average list price of $350,000 and an average sale price of $338,000. Subtract the average sale price from the average list price, then divide the difference by the average listing price. Here's the math: $350,000-$338,000=$12,000; $12,000 divided by the $350,000 =0.034 or a 3.4% markdown.

In other words you should understand that it's normal in your market to expect a market, or discount of 3.4% from the listing price.

You'll also have an advantage in negotiations with other agents when you know the average markdown. Suppose that the average markdown in a certain neighborhood is only .5% while they're offering 4% below the asking price. You can confidently tell the other agent that it's unreasonable to expect that we would accept that price and that he should encourage the client to make a more reasonable offer based on actual market data of list price versus sold price in that neighborhood. I can't tell you how many times this simple formula has saved thousands of dollars for my clients because I knew the market statistics and the other agents did not.

Chapter 9:

Secrets to Effective Pricing

The Guess and Go Agent Analysis is the Most Costly Mistake You Can Make

Let's be completely honest . . . as a listing agent using the traditional method of doing a market analysis or CMA, you can make the numbers say just about anything you want. I know that's a really strong statement, so let me explain.

With the traditional CMA method, the typical agent selects between 3 recently sold properties that are closely comparable to the subject home (or the home being valued). In most markets, it's easy to find 3 properties that sold high, 3 sold low, and 3 that sold somewhere in the middle and still have many other comparables from which to choose. The real problem that exists is the size of the sample.

In statistics there is a common concept known as "margin of error." The margin of error of any sample can be calculated with a simple formula. Margin of error equals 1 divided by the square root of the sample size. For example if you have a sample size of 400, the square root of 400 is equal to 20. One divided by 20 is 1/20th or 5%. Margin of error for a sample size of 400 is 5%.

Why The Guess and Go Can Cost You Thousands

When I teach classes on doing a CMA, I typically walk the class through these calculations on several sample sizes. What if you had 100 in your sample? The margin of error would be 10%. Or a sample of 64? The margin of error in this case would be 12.5% what if you only have a sample size of 16 properties? You got it a margin of error of 25%.

Now what if the sample size had just 3 comparable properties? Margin of error is a glaring 58%! Think about it. Using the traditional method of conducting a CMA, taught by every real estate school and used by just about every real estate broker or agent, you're essentially saying, "Mr. Seller, your home is worth $220,000 . . . plus or minus $129,000!"

Thankfully you're not saying this otherwise you'd never get you home price correctly. But do you see the problem? It is the sample size. When a seller balks after an agent suggests a listing price, the agent immediately retreats and says, "Well, maybe I can try to find some different comparables and get back to you with some more information."

This traditional price method teaches agents to list the home as inexpensively as possible so it will sell quickly.

The Ultimate Comparative Market Analysis

So now that I've destroyed the traditional method of producing CMA let me teach you how I conduct a bulletproof CMA . . .

I take data from 4 different sources to compile the largest sample size that possible, in order to reduce the margin of error and increase the accuracy in pricing a home. The 4 sources I use are:

- County tax records of the original sale price
- Comparable listings in the MLS
- Pending listings in the MLS
- Active comparable listings

Remember, I do this to get the most accurate price possible, with the lowest margin of error, which requires a large sample size.

First I look at the tax records to determine what I feel to be adjusted current value of the home. For example, if it sold 3 years ago for $150,000 and there has been a depreciation rate in the area of 10% and then I subtract that figure from the original purchase price to arrive at an adjusted current value.

How do I find out how much the market has depreciated? That's easy. I take the average sale price for the market for the year the seller bought their home. Then I find the average sale price for the current year using the same sample. If the average sale price for my sample group for year one was $400,000 and the average sale price for this current year is $350,000 then the market has depreciated 12.5% over that period. I then adjust the original purchase price by that amount.

Using the example above $400,000 -12.5% or $50,000 is and depreciation adjusted value of $350,000. Certainly this method alone is not extremely accurate, but it is only the first part of my valuation process.

Next I pull out all the close comparable properties in the area, going back a reasonable period of time. I can usually find 15 to 25 of these.

Don't forget that the amenities, how nice a home, how pretty its' curb appeal is, can affect the salability of the property but will have very little impact on the appraised value, so it is best use as many comparable properties as possible. In selecting my comparables, as I stated before, I use the school district, the square footage and lot size (within a range of + or -20% for square footage and lot size). I then calculate the average sale price of the group, eliminating the low priced properties (examples would include bank owned properties and foreclosures) from my calculation.

Next, I pull up all the pending comparable listings. Again, I use the school district, lot size and the square footage.

And finally, I pull up all the active comparable listings, using the same criteria of school district lot size and square footage. The point is to get as much data as possible!

Now I pull it all together in a spreadsheet. I take the appreciation or depreciation adjusted value from the tax records, at the average price from the close comps, pending comps, and then add the average price from the active comps. Now take that number and divide by 4 and you'll have the true average value for the subject property.

Write down this new number somewhere then add and subtract 5% from this number and you'll have a 10% "reasonable range" for the value of the home, and it's extremely accurate. If you use this method, you will find that you simply cannot get a more accurate valuation.

This method will absolutely stand up under any amount of scrutiny by clients, other agents, or most importantly appraisers. I can tell you from past experience that when you show your valuation to an appraiser or a buyer's agent, they'll have no issues with it. This method will protect you from accidentally overpricing or under pricing any property in any market.

I have found this valuation is as accurate as any certified appraisal, sometimes even more so. Remember an appraiser is just a certified opinion on value that is conducted for specific purpose. That purpose is usually disclosed upfront, whether it be for refinancing or a resale, the appraiser will have access to the real estate contract before writing his formal opinion. The actual market value is the amount a buyer is willing to pay and the amount the seller is willing to sell under normal circumstances.

Never Use AVM's

Be careful about using websites that offer you a computer generated valuation. Websites like Zillow.com and Trulia.com use an "automated valuation model," or AVMs, which aggregate sales data from comparable properties to determine an estimated price. While AVMs can be useful as a benchmark for determining value, they can be off by as much as 20% or more, just like inexperienced real estate agents.

Chapter 10:

Quality Marketing is a Necessary Evil

An Industry Ripe with Marketing Incest

Most agents and FSBO sellers fail to properly market properties effectively, because they suffer from what I call "marketing incest." It is caused by from agents and FSBO sellers only looking for ideas inside their own industry and copying what all other agents and FSBO sellers are doing in their own town, city or state. Their marketing becomes so "inbred" it is no longer effective or efficient, and almost impossible for it to produce any measurable results whatsoever.

Look around. 99% of all real estate property marketing looks identical. It is actually brand advertising, not marketing at all. If you need proof just open any copy of the real estate book you find. On every page, the same-style ad, all competing for the same fish, in the same pond, using the same bait. It is hard to stand out from the crowd that way. In fact when the only difference in each publication is the size of the ad, there is no measurable differentiation you can present.

Consider Your Property a Product Launch

What you need is a better marketing message delivered to a carefully defined and specific target audience. Do this; and you'll have no real competition.

This is strategic buyer marketing, or niche marketing, and it is exactly what I prescribe to all my clients to achieve the best opportunity to sell their home for the highest dollar amount in the least amount of time. The key to my marketing success is what I like to call "active marketing," instead of passive marketing such as open houses or print classified ads (which you know already does not work to sell homes).

It's All About Making a Connection

You cannot "connect" with your prospective
homebuyers effectively without a solid
AND
an intimate understanding of who your potential buyer really, really, REALLY IS!

Having a lack of good marketing ideas and a core marketing message is a result of lazy research syndrome!

It took me years to realize the best copywriters are the most tenacious researchers. A good copywriter knows so much about the product and the prospect's wants, fears, assumptions and lingo that the copy soon wants to burst forth as if a dam is breaking. Research is the infallible cure for writer block. Almost everything is better when sold with a "psychological approach" than with a product approach.

Finding a Quality Buyer

We're going to go through a lot of potential lookers to find a buyer who is ready, able and willing. One in 12 is a general rule of thumb as the benchmark of finding an interested buyer. From this pool of 12 quality showings (not tire kickers, low ballers and serial shoppers), there should be the one, highest, and best user of this property that is ready, able, and willing to pay the highest possible price for the property and close the deal.

Not all buyers are created equal. It is the motivation of a particular buyer that is the main distinction between buyers. The buyer who in a perfect world wants to buy, at his price, but doesn't really have to buy has proven to be one of the greatest time wasters and disappointments. So, understanding their needs and motivation of a buyer will make the rest of the screening process easy. Where there is little motivation, a low offer usually follows.

Where Does a Quality Buyer Come From?

Where do the best buyers come from? This can be determined in large part by looking at past sales in your particular area. The average buyer in my business moves within 13 miles of their previous home and spends 31% more on their next home, I know this because I know the data about my customers and their buying preferences.

Now . . . onto the 8 main sources from which the best buyers are typically found . . .

#1: The person who sold a home, needs to buy a home

These prospects are the best buyers, since they have the highest level of motivation: homelessness. They're moving out of a house soon, because the required by contract to do so. Keeping this in mind, you should consider how you can accommodate their time frame for moving.

Until buyers have truly compared available homes in the market, it's hard for them to make a decision about which home suit them best. So asking any buyer how many homes they have looked at over what period of time is the quickest and most efficient way to determine how ready they are to buy.

Studies have shown among the overwhelming majority of families, the wife does most of the shopping for property and tends to find the house first. The husband, of course, will usually have the power of veto.

My last thought on this type of buyer is that you can't judge a book by its cover. Sometimes, the hardest part of the transaction is setting an appointment for re-showing with all the decision-makers present, getting them off the fence in this uncertain economic climate can still prove to be difficult, even if they are under contract to sell.

#2: From a real estate broker who had customers who lost out on a home to another buyer

I like to call this the "runaway bride syndrome." This is the case when the buyer has, for whatever reason, just lost out when purchasing a home similar to yours because of a better offer from another buyer. Typically, it was higher offer, but it could've been someone more qualified to buy or someone with a more preferable time frame.

Regardless of the circumstances, this buyer in front of you is now ready, willing and able to purchase a home, not to mention strongly motivated to win this time. In this case they know what they want, and they have learned that they are not the only buyer in the market that wants the same thing.

#3: Move up buyers

Families expanding need a larger home, occasionally local contractors can be a great source of these leads. They often deal with families considering making a colossal mistake of over-improving their home for the neighborhood. Eventually, when reality sets in, they realize that moving into a larger home makes more sense.

#4: Tenants who want to stop paying rent

Apartment buildings and condominiums can be a great source of prospective buyers with growing families. Interest rates are currently at historic all-time lows, which makes affordability that much higher.

#5: Empty nesters with big homes who want to downsize

Owners of homes that are obviously much larger than yours and are close in proximity may be the potential buyers for your home. You can purchase a list of people in the proximity of your home who have owned for more than 10 years, try infousa.com

#6: 1031 Exchange buyers

Under section 1031 of the Internal Revenue Code, an investor can sell the property and buy replacement property without paying capital gains tax. IRS rules are technical and beyond the scope of this book, it is safe to say that in your area there are 1031 exchange facilities and you can let them know of your property for sale.

#7: Relocation buyers

Relocation buyers are typically corporate professionals, who relocate due to a better job offer. They typically are high wage earners, with excellent credit scores and steady employment history. However, in the current economic conditions that exist, many corporations fail to offer a buyer a relocation package that includes purchasing their existing home. Many of these buyers have substantial investments in their property that in today's market prove troublesome to sell.

Always be sure to ask the question whether or not they have a home to sell before entertaining an offer from a relocation buyer. It is not advisable in today's market to accept a sale contingency on someone's current property selling that is located outside of the local market. You have little if any ability to gain market data and understand the housing market they are coming from.

#8: Lead sellers who have a prequalified buyer

Websites like Zillow.com, Trulia.com, Realtor.com and Lending Tree.com exist to sell leads to agents and brokers. They typically have warm leads that they sell for a fee to both lenders and real estate agents, usually from one of their numerous websites. They typically prescreen each lead and have verified their contact info and desire to purchase a home. For a fee they will sell the lead to an agent who has a shortage of buyers.

~~~~

Now that you know where leads come from that turn into buyers, you need to understand how to attract quality buyers to your property.
~~~~

Active Marketing to Effectively Dominate

We paid one of the top direct response internet marketing consultants in the country over $10,000 to develop our Ultimate Digital Home Marketing Program. The program includes 45 best-practices elements with well over 400 steps in our Platinum Listing program. *It includes proprietary software and techniques no other agent has access to.* We did this because I truly believe in active marketing does make all the difference.

I will discuss the major elements of this multi-faceted active marketing strategy. Many of the topics warrant a book of their own due to their complexity, but I will still touch on these subjects due to the overall importance of these topics in the challenging market we face.

Are You Selling a Home or a Lifestyle?

The more you know about your desired prospective buyer, the better, more personalized, more accurate, more powerful, more targeted better connection you can make with your potential buyer in your marketing message.

Extraordinary marketers are working to make a connection. Connections are about feelings and emotions. You must get inside the head of the potential home buyer and understand the person that had is being written for, only then can you "connect" effectively. The bottom line is to understand the "who" before attempting to ever sell the "what." Buyers buy on emotion and justify based on logic. To successfully persuade others you must address both sides of the brain:

Left brain = Logic / Right brain = Emotion

Develop a Neighborhood Lifestyle Profile First

All that we do to prepare a listing, from initial research to photos to video to SEO to magnetic copyrighting is done before a property is ever listed in the MLS. It actually takes about 2 weeks to assemble all the assets into a comprehensive marketing launch of your "lifestyle product" (home for sale). The MLS inclusion is actually one of the final steps in our marketing plan. The reason for this is simple: the MLS syndicates the property to all the real estate search sites like Trulia and Zillow and Realtor.com.

Agents have no control over how it is displayed or marketed on these other sites. These sites actually are designed to sell advertising to agents, not sell your home. The only reason to use them is if you have no other means to market your property. In my own practice, I purposely give these sites the info last, to ensure that Google gives us page rank authority as the originators of the content provided. This keeps our original marketing message on top of the search engine results, and gives our clients homes the best chance to shine.

The Advantages of Great Photography

It is a proven fact that photography most definitely does sell real estate. The quality and quantity of photographs offered increases the sale price and decreases the days on market in every study. Buyers quickly use photos as a means to eliminate properties from their "must see" list.

In addition, your home is competing against model homes from builders such as Toll Brothers who have thousands of dollars at their disposal to professionally stage and clean their model homes.

Most real estate agents are too anxious to get your home on the market. Before the ink is dry, they've snapped a few photos with their IPhone and loaded your home into the MLS. Yes, they may get homes on the market faster, but those homes stay on the market longer.

At the James Harner Group, we believe that preparation is absolutely essential in today's market. For that reason, we work with a full suite of professional vendors, professional stagers, repair teams and we even have our own staff real estate photographer and videographer. This ensures that your home shows its' very best, both online and when a buyer walks in the door. The result is that our homes sell faster and for more money, so I recommend you do the same thing when selling your home.

The Two Ways to Great Results

There are two ways to achieve professional results when taking real estate photos and video. The first way is the easiest to implement. If you are not confident with your ability or your agent's ability to take professional pictures, I suggest hiring a professional for professional results. 99% of agents suck at photography and videography. The evidence is clear when you look at what is on real estate websites. YUCK! It looks like most real estate pictures I see were taken by a 5th grader!

The second way to produce quality photography is to understand what makes an excellent real estate photograph so appealing. The secret of professional real estate photographers is *high contrast in the photo composition.* You see, the eye gravitates to the most contrast when viewing photographs. Place 4 pictures next to each other; 1 with high contrast and the other 3 with the sun high in the sky and the eye will always go to the photo with high contrast as the most attractive photo. Professionals know this and that is why their pictures look so much more visual appealing.

With that being said, without going into an advanced photography class, I'll tell you how I achieve excellent results that you can't tell the difference between my pictures and a professional photographer.

The Money Shot is Critical

I like to call the main exterior photo the "money shot." This is the critical picture you have to get right. The interior and other exterior shots will live or die based on the quality of the main photo. It's the one everyone will see as a first impression online and in print. It will create the visual interest to stimulate them to look at the rest of the pictures, but they will always come back to this one.

This "money shot" is composed of the following details:

- It will have a large amount of contrast, which creates the visual appeal.
- There will always be a blue sky.
- It will be taken at what is called the "blue time" in photographer speak. There is an excellent Iphone app to determine when the sun will be in correct position to the front of the house called lighttrac - look for it in the Apple store. It will take the guess work out of knowing when to take the photo.
- Remember to keep the sun always behind you when taking this picture.
- The interior and exterior lights around the home are always turned on (also adds contrast).
- I always use the manual mode with my Nikon DSLR camera. Yes I said a DSLR, you can't

achieve the professional results necessary with a point and shoot camera or your IPhone.

- I always use a tripod.
- You should take the picture from chest height.
- I set the camera's aperture priority to F8 and adjust the white balance to increase the warmth.

That is pretty much it, besides having an eye for the visual right angle to shoot from. Knowing which angle takes a bit of an artistic eye, but just know that you never want to shoot straight on. Always adjust the viewing angle of the shot to show depth, which is photographers trick to fool the eye into thinking the picture is 3 dimensions.

A Videographer Will Sell the Lifestyle

Video is a whole other element that I find 100% necessary in order to properly market a home. YouTube and many other video sites are hugely visited by home buyers. Again, people are visual creatures, they need to see it first, and again statistics show that the more video you provide in marketing the property, the higher the sale price and the quicker it will sell. It will get you more overall looks from prospective buyers and increase the likelihood of effective showings that will result in a sale.

We use an Ipad2 with a wide angle lens along with a secondary light source to illuminate the interior scenes.

I use video as another way to tell the story of the home in short clips. When edited together in IMovie the result is a 4-5 minute video that gives the viewer all the necessary information to make an intelligent decision on whether this home has the necessary elements and the neighborhood lifestyle elements of to make a showing worthwhile.

If you must, again hire a professional to do this for you if you or your agent can't do this type of creative work.

Story telling is critical to success with video.

Viral Video Marketing Can Improve Your Chances

Once a video is created, promoting it to the internet is key to actively market the property. We use proprietary web based software called "HUTTBUZZ" to market videos and photos.

What is Huttbuzz you ask? It is a comprehensive program designed to Search Engine Optimize (SEO) photos and videos for a particular property address, adds chosen key-phrases AND at the same time promotes the client's home while driving internet traffic to Lead Generation pages where ever possible. It has a cumulative effect of an 800 pound gorilla with a sledgehammer to the search engines!

Video sites like Youtube and Wistera are gaining increased relevance in the search engine placement game, and original content is king. With this in mind, we have achieved success few agents can match in gaining exposure of our listings to the buying public. Our process will outmuscle all the others including Trulia.com and Zillow.com fighting for the top spot and assure your home gets first page ranking on Google, which is the only search engine that even matters.

With a little research and learning on your part, should you decide to sell your house yourself, you can easily just go on line to learn about Huttbuzz and SEOs. As you will read below, I even will teach you how to do it!

The Benefits of Search Engine Optimization

Most Realtors or the public in general have no clue on where to even begin to obtain page one ranking on Google. Google highly values original content by original authors. By understanding this and optimizing the video and photos for the correct key-phrases, specifically for the individual listing, it is possible to achieve page one rankings. This will produce targeted buyer traffic for your home.

I have done this more times than I can count and have sold many listings within weeks, after other agents had failed to do so while on the market for years. This is my silver bullet. If you want to use HUTTBUZZ, contact me for training and pricing. This is an advanced topic, so a thorough understanding of SEO is necessary to get these kinds of results.

Below are the unique strategies we deploy with this unique HUTTBUZZ technology.

Unique Strategy #1. Call to Action Home Photos: This means that when we create a property listing for syndication and promotion we will embed other graphics and calls to action in the photos, in the text, and if on a webpage, in the sidebar.

Unique Strategy #2. A key component of our promotion is to tightly integrate our client's single property website and systems with Google Apps, Google Plus, and Facebook for SEO (social search) purposes and viral marketing.

Unique Strategy #3. Social Proof Building via Google+, Facebook and Twitter using the Huttbuzz system is critical for SEO and lead capture purposes.

Unique Strategy #4. We will also be promoting the properties first, in order to ensure our content gets author rank FIRST by search engines so we don't bleed traffic and leads to huge authority sites like Zillow and Trulia. This ensures are message is not watered down.

Unique Strategy #5. We will also syndicate the same property through multiple channels (with tiny address or other changes if necessary) so that it will show up multiple times in Property Search Aggregation sites like Zillow and Trulia.

Social Media Marketing

Social networking has taken off and is helping us sell homes. It is a critical component to the HUTTBUZZ SEO campaign, called social proof building. Google has shown that it gives strong weight to these social share sites as original and authoritative, thus providing us with first page on Google results for our listings. Each new listing we advertise a social proof campaign is created in HUTTBUZZ and is broadcast through thousands of other social members to promote the listings though Google+, Facebook and Twitter. The cumulative effect is to get Google to rank the property business page on page 1.

It works.

In addition, we post the listing business page that is created for your property on our business page for the specific community (we have 8, each of which is for a different area we serve). We also instruct our clients to like the business page we create for the listing and have them send all their friends and family to like it.

What is Blogging and Why is it Important?

Blogging is a new form of online journalism. It has taken the web by storm, and our blog is ranked on page 1 for Philadelphia homes for sale, which is a top searched keyword in the real estate market. Creating a targeted blog post, specifically designed to make a connection to the reader about your home and optimizing it for SEO is an extremely effective and successful medium for online marketing.

"Pay Per Click" is Targeted Marketing

Pay per click (PPC) advertising is unlike any other form of advertising, because the recipient of the ads determines if and when an ad is paid for. A skillfully managed PPC campaign for a property listing can be a cheap and effective way to generate buyer leads and sell a property quickly. It is so effective because you are only marketing to those individuals who are seeking what you are offering, and you only pay when they respond.

I only use Adwords campaigns on Google. I'm able to monitor the advertising expenses on real time. No more wondering if an ad is working. The key to success is two- fold:

- First, you must be able to write an interesting PPC ad that contains the keywords for which you want to be found.

- Second, you must provide just enough information to the prospect in order to capture their contact information - which is why the competition crusher website is a key component to the success of this program for us!

Competition Crusher Website

This product offers some unique features like a unique website address based on your property's address. We include all your homes details. We add the Facebook likes for your home and comments for social proof. We add in a unique buyers incentive to inquire through the website, which may save the seller some commission. We include a live chat window and a lead capture form.

It is like a single property website on steroids and helps to ensure the buyer leads come thru our team which can reduce the commission paid at closing by allowing us to spend less money marketing the property and decrease the time it takes to sell.

The Benefits of Broadcast Email Marketing

I find email marketing to agents as an extremely effective way of promoting a property, and more specifically, the commission being offered. I purchase broadcast email packages from a local email vendor for the target area of my listing to send a highlight sheet to. I always promote the high commission split to agents, along with a "money shot" photo to generate buzz for my listing. Remember, agents sell listings at least 40% of the time, so using email to market to their pocketbooks is an effective way to bribe them to show our listing. The chances of another agent selling our listings are much greater than us selling it on our own.

Mobile & Eco Friendly Marketing

A mobile texting solution tied to a sign rider is an excellent and Eco friendly way to promote your property to prospective buyers when they are driving by your listing. They enter a specific code and send a text message to the number listed on the sign, they are they sent the property info in a mobile smart phone friendly readable flyer. The additional benefit of using a lead capture system like this is that the phone number of the prospect is captured and you can call them. I recommend this over flyer boxes at listings.

~~~~~

These are the most effective cutting edge marketing solutions I wanted to share. In addition, we also deploy many company provided solutions for additional active marketing benefits including listing syndication to over 80 real estate sites. We utilize preferred first page placement on Zillow, Trulia and Realtor.com. We
~~~~~

conduct daily Craigslist posting. We provide virtual tours. In addition a traditional single property website via realbird.com. is an effective means of generating long-term interest, since the listing information does not die once the listing has been sold.

You must think I am crazy for sharing all of my secrets with you, but I believe that if you want to sell your house on your own, that is fine. But I want you to be successful. And if you are hiring a traditional salesperson, that is fine too. But in both cases, you need to watch out for your wallet. We absolutely guarantee that our Platinum Listing Program does more to sell a home, with your goals in mind than any other agent, team or brokerage in the entire country without question, so I honestly believe you are getting the best information available to put more money in your pocket and sell your home the fastest way possible.

Chapter 11:

Finding a Market Expert (if you must!)

Should I Do It Myself?

Certainly. I would highly recommend selling your home by yourself and pocketing that commission if market conditions are such that it makes sense for you to do so, as discussed in the FSBO chapter number 6. But the reality is that most of the time, that's not the case.

Statistically, 91% of FSBO sellers never sell their own homes. Is it because they are not motivated? No. Is it because they don't want to spend money to actively market their homes? No. Is it because they lack the necessary specific marketing skills? Maybe. Is it because they lack specific skills like contract law, qualification of potential buyers, or negotiation of an acceptable contract? No. No. No.

The reason most FSBO sellers are unsuccessful is because the market is not favorable for the FSBO strategy.

When market conditions are right, selling your own home is a great way to go, but when the market is a buyer's market, strategy simply just does not work. And what makes matters worse is that in the process many would-be FSBO sellers lose valuable time and incur a great deal of financial loss (months of additional payments, advertising costs, and the stigmatism of a home that sits on the market and buyers wonder what is wrong with it). Not to mention the emotional stress arguments and worrying and of trying to go it alone in the wrong market wondering what is going wrong. UGH!

Do I Have Time to Properly Market My Home?

Another concern that may influence the decision whether or not to go FSBO is whether or not you really have the time to market your own property properly. As you read in the previous chapter, a successful marketing package will take some time to set up, especially if you are a newbie at selling a home.

Also ask yourself, "Do I want to go to the trouble of marketing the home myself if I can find a competent agent that will do it better and more than pay for his own brokerage fee?"

Clearly, the only one who can make that decision is you, the seller. In most cases, the smart money is on hiring a highly skilled and professional listing agent - a competent and highly skilled marketing specialist well-versed in copywriting, photography, videography, and search engine optimization not to mention highly skilled at negotiation and contract law. But if you don't select a competent agent, you're probably better off doing it yourself.

You may be thinking, "How can I select and hire a competent agent in the virtual sea of mediocre agents?" That's a great question. Don't hire someone because he or she is a friend of the family or he or she is a relative or someone your go to church with. This is a business decision, with large financial implications, and as such you should treat it as one.

How to Compare Agents

It comes down to two things:

- First, you need an agent who knows your market like the back of their hand.
- Second, the agent needs to be able to understand you, your needs, and specific situation and be able to implement a specific marketing plan in conjunction with a traffic approach. Many agents are not willing to allow you to dictate the marketing approach and they will insist on using the age-old tired price approach.

If you decide to interview an agent and he is not able to both demonstrate his knowledge of your market and a willingness to break away from the traditional way of selling homes, you need to find another agent. That sounds harsh, I know, but the sale of your home has a huge financial and emotional impact on you and your family. Do not be afraid to acknowledge this and just say no thank you and keep on shopping for a better agent.

If you hire an agent, they must be willing to work for you and you only. Here's what I mean by that . . .

This is your home. You are the one deciding how best to sell. You need to hire an agent who will be willing to break from the traditional mold and use an active marketing approach. If you hire an agent that's not willing to try this approach he won't put his heart into marketing the property and spends time looking for buyers, you'll be doing all the hard work yourself by price marketing.

Your agent should be contacting every other buyer's agent in your market on a weekly basis, via email and phone. Top agents have a database of all agents in the marketplace, inclusive of phone numbers and e-mail addresses, and can easily communicate with them to remind them of the additional commission that is available to the buyer's agent bringing a successful contract to closing. If your agent fails to follow through on that part of the approach, it will be much tougher to get great results.

Remember, the whole reason for using an agent is to have access to the other agents in the market. Agents sell houses, so you need to direct a substantial portion of your advertising budget directly at them.

You shouldn't hire an agent because he or she is a “gazillion dollar” producer or has lots of alphabet soup real estate designations listed after their name. Don’t be sold by fancy brochures, slick marketing pieces, slick business cards or PowerPoint presentations. The size of the agents company is irrelevant. So is whether or not they are with a national franchise. None of those things will get you top dollar for your home if all his marketing is "you’ll love me" advertising.

The Checklist for Finding a Local Expert

The agent you hire should be able to do the following:

- ✓ Clearly demonstrate his knowledge of your real estate market.
- ✓ Give you accurate DOM data.
- ✓ Give you accurate sales probability.
- ✓ Give you accurate listing to final sale price ratios to determine average markdown

- ✓ Give you accurate absorption rate data to determine the accurate days on market.
- ✓ Have specialized active marketing plans for reaching other agents in your local market.
- ✓ Market the property to every potential buyer using the niche marketing techniques I have discussed.
- ✓ Know what the local market appreciation or depreciation rates have been over the last several years.
- ✓ Know what to expect in the way of" normal" discounts in the current market.

In other words they should clearly know your market inside and out, front to back, no excuses. Even if he is a great agent, if they're not knowledgeable when it comes to your specific market, they're not your Guy or Gal.

This is your house - take the time to find the best agent for you, your family and your specific situation.

Beware of the One Size Fits All Approach

Highly specialize listing programs are the best way to accommodate your specific needs. Beware of any agent offering a one-size fits all approach. Our team has created and offers several unique strategies to accommodate your specific selling needs. As an example of what you should look for, here are some examples of what we offer:

Up Sell Your Home Platinum Program. We are able to maximize your homes sale price with a comprehensive 401 point marketing program that includes all aspects of the home marketing and presentation, and includes a certification process, backed with a checklist of inspections and a bumper to bumper 12 month full home warranty for buyer confidence after the sale and seller protection.

International Fine Homes Program. Our exclusive internationally recognized marketing program for homes valued at over 1 million dollars. Our Luxury Listing Marketing Program was designed by one of the top internet marketing experts in the country (at a cost to us of over $10,000.) The 45 strategies and 401 steps are valued at $21,519 for the first month and $5,750 for additional months.

Care Free Listing Program. Most brokers charge the same fee no matter how your home sells. With the Care Free listing you have complete flexibility, from full service to "do it yourself".

Early Bird Listing Program. Most home buyers start their search at least 6 months prior to getting serious about buying a home. We will advertise your home on 1,000 websites so these searchers can see it - but tell them that there are NO Showings until you are ready to sell. You'll have a ready and waiting pool of buyers.

Short Sale Solutions Program. Our company exclusive litigation team provides a dedicated team of negotiators and loss mitigation specialists. Their insider knowledge of every bank and lender will get your short sale approved in record time. We will get your short sale to the closing table.

Auction Program. Our affiliation with the Sheldon Good & Company Auctioneers, the Gold Standard of real estate auction houses, will provide you the quickest, most effective method of exposing your property to a large pool of national buyers and investors.

If you don't know an agent that can provide these criteria, feel free to call me and I'll be happy to help you find one. I know agents worldwide. My contact information is in the "about the author" section in the back of this book, and someone will be able to take your call any business.

I've had over 9000 agents worldwide take my listing seminar and have learned active marketing approach, so I'm generally able to match up a seller with a competent agent using these advanced techniques.

Remember, the right agent can make his commission back to you several times over. Don't be penny wise and dollar foolish. Find a top-notch agent.

Chapter 12:

Cooperation

The Principal of Reciprocity

As previously stated, all buyers agents are 100% commission based salespeople. They only get paid when they bring a buyer to the settlement table. When they can deliver a buyer and receive a great reward than other properties are offering, you've got a great incentive for mutual cooperation to get the deal done.

And as I have shown, you can still achieve up to an 10% greater price using this method and do so much faster. We've all heard the age old adage of what goes around, comes around. It is true. In others words, GIVE, and it will be given back to you. This principal is true in two different ways:

- The more you do to help others, the more your kindness and generosity will come back to you. Giving abundantly is the key to success in your ventures.
- If you want to reap success, you need to sow success for those around you.

This being said, don't waste time thinking that lowering the commission is the way to get the most money. It is the opposite of the reality you are faced with.

You actually need those buyer agents – think of them as your employees, or as partners even. Even though not every buyer will have a buyer's agent, the truth is that most of them will. Plus, it is MUCH easier to deal directly with the buyer's agent than with the buyer themselves.

- Buyers want to get your house for as little as possible; buyer's agents want to get paid.
- Buyers are highly emotional, making it difficult to negotiate; buyer's agents do not have any emotional attachment to your home (except for the commission you are going to pay them!
- Buyer's are under stress – for some reason they HAVE to move; buyer's agents are used to performing under stress.

In addition, if you choose to sell on your own, then you can utilize the buyer agent to help with the paperwork.

Do remember though, a buyer's agent, by law, works for and represents the buyer, not you.

If you hire an agent to help you sell your home, you do get some great benefits, but only if you hire the right one. They are responsible for a whole slew of things, some of which are:

- All the paperwork (hundreds of pieces of paper throughout the whole sale of your home).
- Researching the right price for your home.
- Marketing your home.
- Communicating with all the buyer agents.
- Communicating with you.
- Communicating with all of the service providers involved in a real estate sale (inspectors, bankers, appraisers, etc.)
- Effective negotiation

The commission you pay to “cooperate” with these agents is worth its’ price – but only if you hire the right agent, or if you re FSBOing, then only if you bribe the buyer’s agent with a nice sized commission.

Chapter 13:

Negotiation

The Art of Persuasion and Trade

The goal of this chapter is to provide increased negotiation skills, tools, approaches and techniques for negotiating better outcomes and gaining a higher level of negotiation knowledge separate yourself from your competition and get the results you desire.

There are many different negotiations conducted routinely in real estate. Real estate clients expect a real estate agent to be knowledgeable and negotiation approaches and techniques, NAR's 2011 profile of home buyers and sellers shows the disparity in expectations vs. results:

- 99% of buyers believe negotiation skills are "very important" (page 65)
- only 44% of all buyers felt their agent "negotiated a better contract outcome" (page 63)
- buyers give "negotiation skills" the lowest satisfaction rating of all agent skills and qualities (page 66)

- only 5% of sellers want "help with negotiating"

The questions that arise from these statistics are obvious.

Why are buyers not satisfied with their agent's negotiation outcomes?

Why do only 5% of sellers look for negotiation skills in their agent?

When this is the most important financial transaction most people ever have, wouldn't having someone possessing the tools of a highly skilled negotiator be of a great benefit? Then why do less than 1% of agents nationwide take the time to learn this necessary skill-set? This fact blows my mind. I often feel like I bring a bazooka to a knife fight when dealing with most agent's ability to negotiate. They give away the farm and all I have to do is ask!

Knowledge and Planning are the Foundation

The negotiation model I have been taught is based on the The Harvard Business Schools foundation of collaborative win - win thinking. The two major foundations are knowledge and planning. Through knowledge, obtained through the proper gathering and interpretation of information, is used with the systematic planning approach to identify and select appropriate options. Conscious and effective use of professional influence approaches and tactics that help achieve a win - win outcome is proper planning when entering into a negotiation.

Four Key Habits of Successful Negotiators

Negotiation is an information game. The better you are at obtaining information, the better you can potentially negotiate a successful outcome. The best negotiators exhibit 4 key habits throughout the negotiation process.

1. A willingness to properly prepare and conduct research
2. High expectations for a favorable outcome
3. Patience to listen to opposing views, without becoming emotional.
4. Commitment to personal integrity

The Three Critical Stages of Every Negotiation

There are three stages that every negotiation must pass through. We will discuss these three critical stages and strategies on how you can gain the upper hand and still provide a win/win outcome for all parties. Remember, not everyone wants the same thing and the way that you create value effects how it gets divided. When you voluntarily provide a concession, it provides the greatest principle for reciprocity.

1. Establishing criteria (what exactly do "they" want)

2. Get all the information you possibly can
3. Reaching for a compromise

Establishing Criteria

By asking questions, to establish what in fact the other side wants, then repeating their statements to confirm what has been stated and summarizing their position, you have effectively let the other side know that you understand their position. I always recommend starting from this place, because it shows a patience to listen and understand. Creating good will goes a long way towards creating a successful outcome for both parties.

Information Gathering

Skilled negotiators gather information by asking questions, repeating statements as questions, confirming or summarizing your understanding of what is said and asking third parties. There are several ways to ask questions: open-ended questions, closed-end questions speculative questions, "tell me…", "Describe to me…", "Help me understand…"

The more information you can gather at this stage, the better you will be prepared to provide solutions to the other buyer's problems, and create a win/win outcome. Uncovering what is truly important to the other side allows you to put together a solution that addresses your clients needs AND the other party's needs.

7 Strategies for Reaching Compromise

There are 7 key success persuasion strategies to utilize when entering into negotiation. We will discuss these individually below.

Success Persuasion Negotiation Approaches

S Self Interest

U Uniqueness

C Contrast

C Communication

E Exchange

S Sameness

S Sound Logic

- *Self Interest Principle* is a great starting strategy when beginning to negotiate. What is in their self-interest to do what I want them to do? An excellent example of this is:

What have you gained if prices decline but the interest rates keep rising? You will actually be not better off, but the bank will.

- *The Uniqueness Principle* emphasizes the unique opportunity that exists. People want something more if it is unique, limited or scarce. Offer something special and articulate it's great value. As example would be: This opportunity doesn't come around very often. You can't lose the chance to get a very good deal by waiting for something you won't know until after the fact, when it's already too late.
- *The Contrast Principle* shows that the more reasonable you appear to be, the better the chances exist for getting what you want. By comparing something YOU want with something that makes your choice look infinitely better. Magnify the contrast but be realistic to not appear to be reaching.
- *The Communication Principle* includes words, voice and body language. Effective communication must include all three forms to maximize persuasiveness. The words you say only communicate 10% of your position. Your tone is 25% of your position and your body language is 65%!!!!. Body language proves a very good case for negotiating in person.
- *The Exchange Principle* illustrates what can we trade or exchange of equal value between parties? In business transactions, it is normal to exchange

or trade items of value to reach an agreement. There is a sense of obligation to " give when getting". This can be utilized for mutual benefit. Always get when you give, and consider giving first to "position" your opponent. An example of this is: If you make an offer today on this house, the seller has authorized me to tell you they will give you X,XXX dollars of the price and an allowance of X,XXX in assistance just like you ask for; but it's only good for a deal written today.

- *The Sameness Principle* shows that people like to do business with people who are like them, with people they like, or people they want to be associated with. Find a connection and use it to create camaraderie. Always try to avoid the law of relative separation, which states that people of a group feel it's us against them.

An example of this is: I live in this neighborhood too. I know all the neighbors, my kids go to the same elementary school. I think you'll find this is an ideal home for your family, just like I found out after living here.

- *The Sound Logic Principle* shows that people are more persuaded by a sound, logical position than by an opinion. The tighter the logic the more persuasive you will be. What evidence or logic exists (after gathering information) and makes sense for them to agree with me?

  Example: Look at market fluctuations as your friend rather than your enemy; profit from the folly of others rather than participate in it or not getting in the market today would be like finding a $100 dollar bill on the ground and not picking it up.

What If There is a Deadlock?

The final word on negotiation is BATNA.

What is BATNA you ask?

This is an acronym for the "Best Alternative to a Negotiated Agreement". It is the proper preparation to knowing how far you are willing to bend before breaking off negotiations. Having a clear understanding of what is the sellers walk away point, is an asset. Having this conversation establishes the size of the negotiation playing field and eliminates any frustrations of feeling unsure of the outcome.

An example goes like this: At what price point would your buyer be willing to continue to rent instead of purchasing this home?

Dealing with Different Types of Negotiators

There are 2 main types of Negotiators we will discuss them , how to spot them, the techniques they use and how to position yourself when dealing with them below.

Welcome to Fight Club

Competitive Negotiators have a win/lose mindset. Negotiating with them is like a boxing match of punches, jabs and ducks and blocks. They focus on positions vs. areas of concern. They are interested in dividing the asset like a "fixed" pie mentality. They attempt to negotiate each element separately. They exhibit fewer concessions, abuse power in the negotiation and deliberately hide information. Somctimes they will even use aggressive language to intimidate the other side and are prone to argue over power.

The bottom line, competitive negotiators are easy to spot and hard to please. There are no rules when dealing with them and I do not trust them. In dealing with them I always try to uncover their real interests by diffusing their one track mind and taking them into diffusing questioning away from the negotiation. I use sound logic to defend my clients position. I always try to create " packages" that satisfy both sides and thwart their ability to negotiate items separately. I won't take any abuse and I always guard my information carefully. I will call them on their hard bargaining tactics. I always know my clients walk away point and I am willing to articulate it to them. I will walk away and rescind the offer if the situation warrants this action.

Their competitive tactics include:

- ✓ Low ball/high ball
- ✓ Red Herring (misdirection)
- ✓ Nibbling
- ✓ Intimidation
- ✓ Short Deadlines
- ✓ Bluffing

Building Bridges to Success

Collaborative negotiators have a win/win mindset. They focus on interests vs. a hard and fast stand. They are willing to explore alternatives. They always try to make the pie bigger before dividing it. They are willing to bundle elements into a package and negotiate it collectively. They are willing to share power and are interested in building a trusting relationship. A collaborative negotiator will ask more questions, test for understanding of the other sides position. They will summarize and make positive comments to foster cooperation. They are willing to explore options and test the limits of the terms.

Tactics Used by Collaborative Negotiators

- ✓ Understanding the other sides needs
- ✓ Willingness to explore options
- ✓ Considerate silence
- ✓ Provide reasonable deadlines
- ✓ Follow the Fairness Doctrine
- ✓ Exhibit positive emotions
- ✓ Create exchanges
- ✓ Build trust to establish a relationship
- ✓ Put it in writing
- ✓ Use proven persuasion techniques

Key Components to Remember

- Accumulate all the information you can. No two people want the same thing, so never assume they want what your client wants.
- Collaborate to share power in the negotiation. Never argue with people. Use the feel, felt, found formula. Never narrow negotiation down to one thing. Never negotiate out of emotion. Create a

win/win solution that can address the goals of buyer and seller at the same time.

- Always remember the way in which you create value effects how it is divided.
- Competitively negotiate if collaboration fails. Develop walk away power and effectively communicate this to the other side.
- Execute using persuasion techniques
- BATNA- Know you walk away point if all other strategies fail. Remember you always must represent your client's self-interest and goals first and foremost!

Negotiation Takeaway

By understanding the other sides wants, needs and motivational triggers, gathering information about the them and then carefully utilizing one of these 7 persuasion techniques you can strategically negotiate a win/win outcome for all parties. The alternative to this win/win negotiation is encountered when you must negotiate with a competitive negotiator and then you must know your walk away point and articulate it to the other side and be prepared to rescind the offer if the situation warrants it.

Professional negotiation skills are a must for all real estate agents helping home sellers, especially in the current market. Armed with professional negotiation skills, skilled agents are able to help clients obtain better results in the sale of their home. These agents have a *powerful* competitive edge because of their ability to:

- ✓ Communicate effectively to uncover more information
- ✓ Help clients understand their options
- ✓ Work collaboratively with others
- ✓ Resolve deadlocks

Chapter 14:

Real Life Examples

Finally, I'd like to share some cases where using the active marketing approach has produced great results. Here are a few of my favorite cases from countless times I've used this approach and past.

Through my website, a client who was a licensed real estate agent (noticed I said WAS) in Media, Pennsylvania, approached me one day. His parents had passed away, and because of his real estate experience, siblings had chosen him to help sell the family home. So he called largest company entire market, which happened to be Coldwell Banker, who had listed the home for $264,900. Over the course of 2 years, Coldwell Banker systematically reduced the price to $249,900. But even though it was a very nice house, the seller hadn't received a single offer on it during the course of that were separate listing contracts.

When I explained my idea to the agent, I could see the light come on in his mind! As a previous agent, he intuitively knew this approach would work, so at my suggestion we raised the price to $270,000 and commission from 5.5% to 8%. Well, within a month we have received 3 offers! The first 2 we turned down, but the third was a full price offer and we accepted it.

We had one more hurdle to get past: the appraisal had to support the sale price. As it turned out, the appraisal came in short, and my client had to sell the home for $269,500 and do some minor repairs that amounted to less than $1600 (and probably would've had to be done with any sale at any price).

So after raising the price $20,100 and then paying an extra $6,777.50 (the 2.5% extra commission), my client netted an extra $12,822.50 more money and got the absolute top dollar for his childhood home. Even more importantly, we accomplished in under 90 days what he failed to do into full years: we got offers and were able to command the maximum price because of the traffic generated by the higher commission.

Was he happy? He was thrilled! And so was I.

This is another story you'll love. Again I have a client approached me through my website www.PAHouseQuest.com (are you noticing a trend here?).

This fellow is very frustrated because he bought a brand-new home, closed on it, and was having to make 2 house payments every month. He tried to sell his old house FSBO, and although he shown it a lot, no offers have materialized. Then he listed it was a local brokerage, but the home received no offers and have very few showings.

After the listing expired, I went to see him and showed him my approach, and he decided to try it based on faith in me. We raised the price from $279,900 to $295,000 and immediately a surge showing traffic came through. In exactly 17 days, we sold the home for $295,000.

As in the previous story, we then anxiously waiting for the appraisal, but this time it went through without a hitch this day, my client thinks that I'm a genius and sends me business every chance he gets.

So let's do the math on this edition of commission cost him $6,380. The additional price he was able to command was $15,100, and is net gain was $8,720, or over 3% more money! Best of all, the house sold almost immediately!

I can go on and on with these stories, but I will share just one more . . .

This client was one of those know it all people who thinks he understands real estate better than a professional top producing agent. I approached them with both options (the price approach and the traffic approach), as I always do. His initial reaction was that he'd never heard of the traffic approach and was skeptical because he had a problem with the high commission.

This type of person thinks that real estate agents are hardly worth 3% much less 8%. So we initially listed the home at 7% (let me remind you that we are in a 6% or less market), and we waited. We had a slightly better than average number of showings, but nothing outstanding and no offers for about four months.

Eventually, though, client began to get frustrated and called me to ask what I thought he should do. He was in a hurry to sell the home and have a lot of equity, so he listed it for $246,000. I asked him if he remembered what I've suggested when he first listed the house, and he said "not really."

Then I reminded him that I suggested that we price the home at $256,000 and put commission at 8%. He had been considering reducing the price and was naturally stunned when I told him to raise it. Well, we closed not long afterward! He was very thankful for my getting top dollar, and I can promise you that he will never sell another home same old way.

Quickly looking at the math, you can see that we raise the commission 1% or $2560 and we commanded $10,000 more for the home and sold almost immediately.

~~~~~~

Now, did I do anything different in any of those cases? Absolutely not! I always advertise all my listings exactly the same way and show no preferential treatment, regardless of price or commission rate of the listing.

Remember: advertising does not sell houses; agents do!

What sold those homes and many, many more just like them, was an increased commission. It really is that simple. It is supply and demand, and agents are all commission-based sales persons. Combine that with the fact that the average agent selling less than 10 homes a year, they jump at receiving a higher commission rate. For them it is essentially like getting a raise every time you get paid.

Well there you have it, my active marketing approach in a nutshell to selling homes, for more money and faster than any other traditional agent. It's made me one of the top agents in the country, and, more importantly, it has made my clients some of the happiest in the world! Will
~~~~~~

my systems and ideas work for you? I say unequivocally, absolutely YES!

I have agents and sellers using this very strategy in every corner of the country- even around the world - all receiving the same or similar results. The real question is do you have the courage trust your own instincts? You really can take control of the sale of your home! Seriously, you can. The power is back in your hands.

Remember the movie," Field of Dreams"? The voice from the sky said, "If you build it, they will come." I say that in real estate, the voice is saying, "If you bribe them, they will come." Go ahead . . . what do you have to lose? It costs you nothing to try this approach. NOT trying it can cost you thousands of dollars, months of stress and arguments, and maybe even potentially losing your home if you are financially strapped. Come on. Give it a try.

And when it works (and it always does), then send me an e-mail or a lctter. I look forward to adding your stories to my collection.

About the Author

Author, speaker, globetrotter, syndicated columnist, real estate broker and team leader of The James Harner Group, James Harner is not your typical real estate guru. In an industry dominated by negative public perceptions- where real estate agents are often referred to as undertrained and overpaid, this particular real estate agent runs a "homeowner friendly" outfit and helps area homeowners increase the profits from the sale of their home substantially.

Unlike many of today's "experts" Harner is personally involved in the real estate business on a daily basis. His business objective is to leverage the power of technology, social media, efficient systems and motivated people, resulting in superior results for his clients. He provides home sellers with a proven and repeatable system, backed by market research and consistently sells homes for up to 18% more money in 47% less time than traditional real estate agents.

In 1992, James earned a Bachelor of Arts Degree in Marketing and Business Administration from the

University of Washington's distinguished Michael G. Foster School of Business. Before becoming a top producing real estate agent, James co-founded an international import and export company called the Kind Association. As the C.E.O. of The Kind Association®, he traveled the world pioneering the concept of a fair trade retailer, marketing quality handmade jewelry and home furnishings from skilled artisans to retailers around the world. The marketing and public relations skills that James gained in this arena are instrumental in continuing to build his client-focused boutique style real estate business.

While C.E.O. of The Kind Association®, James occupied his spare time buying, remodeling and selling real estate as an investor. James combined his passion of home craftsmanship and marketing and eventually he realized that real estate was his true passion and career interest.

James Harner has extensive, first-hand experiencc in Pennsylvania real estate from all perspectives as a longtime buyer, seller, investor, property manager and eventually as a licensed real estate broker. His breadth of knowledge lends his clients a uniquely informed insider edge in the local real estate market. At the age of 24 James bought, renovated and began managing his first multi-family investment property in West Chester, PA. Since then, James has successfully invested in real estate and managed properties for 15-plus years for many investors, as well as his own. In 2003 James listed 107 homes during his second year in the business and did $8 million in sales production, where the average sales price was only $147,000. By his third year in real estate, at the age of 32, his single agent practice had grown to become the top producer at the former brokerage where James held his license. James currently holds his real estate broker's license with Prudential Fox and Roach Realtors in the Main Line Philadelphia real estate market.

A lifelong resident of the greater Philadelphia area, Harner is a financial supporter of Habitat for Humanity and Project Outreach. He is a member of the Pennsylvania American Legion. His mother drives bus for the Multi- Services of Pennsylvania, and he lives locally (in Upper Providence) with his wife Carrol and two children Austin and Rylee.

Although he keeps an incredibly busy schedule, he invites his readers to contact him online or by phone with any questions or comments. His phone number is (484)727-8378 and his email address is james@jamesharnergroup.com.

Made in the USA
Monee, IL
04 November 2026

67374666R00085